Revitalizing Congregations

REFOCUSING AND HEALING THROUGH TRANSITIONS

William O. Avery

Foreword by Loren B. Mead

An Alban Institute Publication

Library of Congress Card Number 2002109028

ISBN 1-56699-267-2

For Kathleen D. Avery

Amor con amor se paga

(Love begets love)

Contents

Foreword

Everyone I know who is part of a religious congregation wants to change it. Almost no one is satisfied with it as it is.

This is a strange truth I have come to after looking at hundreds, perhaps thousands, of individual congregations, and after talking to clergy, lay people, bishops, and executives.

Of course, the problem is that there is usually no consensus about *how* people want congregations changed—what they want to get rid of, what they would like to keep, and what they would like to see added. That problem is made more difficult because most congregations also have long-standing patterns of life ("The way we do things around here!") and are notoriously slow to change. It is also very hard to reach consensus on how things got the way they are. Memories differ, and grudges hang around for a long, long time.

This is the bad news of congregational life and leadership, but it is also important good news. Bad, because it is devilishly difficult to change something when people are not sure what they want to change. But good, indeed immensely good, in that in every congregation I know of, people feel some genuine unrest and want the congregation to be "better"—by whatever standards those individuals or groups hold. Every congregation has some energy and desire to make things better.

In my heart, I think of this as a divine discontent that awakens that congregation to better understanding of mission, deeper commitment to building community and making a difference in the lives of members and the broader community. That restlessness is one of the reasons I have hope about congregations and why I like working with them. But how can that "divine discontent" be used to move a congregation toward effective change? That's the big question.

As I look around the religious institutions I know, I see basically three assumptions about the leadership needed for this process, and these assumptions seem to produce models that rule the way we act. Those three models are (1) the great man theory (forgive me the sexist name, but that is how it is thought of by historians), (2) the technological model, and (3) the dialogical team model.

I have seen all of these models work pretty well in some places— sometimes spectacularly well, and I have seen all of them fail. Equally spectacularly. None seems to work everywhere; what works best in any situation seems to depend on the people and the context. Effective leadership seems to be contextual, growing out of the unique history of each congregation. Let me describe them and tell you why I think William Avery can help you think about change where you are.

The great man—or great leader—theory assumes that creative change requires a great, powerful, charismatic leader (like the "man on horseback" the French thought Louis Napoleon was). The belief is that this great person, by dint of personal power, can bring the disparate groups together and forge a path to the future. This person will bring such a compelling vision that all doubts will be dissolved, and all will be clear and possible. Tolstoy (in *War and Peace*) and many others have questioned this thesis.

I see this theory at work in religious institutions whenever there is a leadership role to be filled, for example, as pastor, seminary president or dean, or judicatory executive or staff member. And I want to say I have seen it work. I know an educator who took over leadership of a moribund theological seminary, one that was on the edge of bankruptcy and loss of accreditation, and he turned it around within 10 years. I've seen three-quarters dismantled congregations turn into megachurches under the inspiration of a powerful, charismatic leader. Of course, in both cases others helped, but one cannot gainsay the powerful influence of the great leader.

I guess my overwhelming feeling about this model of church leadership, however, is envy and discouragement. When I have tried charisma, it has not worked for me. I do not instinctively know what buttons to push. Most of the people I see who try to be the great leader end up being poor copies of somebody else. I also find that most congregations seeking great leaders feel angry and disappointed when they discover the clay feet of the leader. If a leader can pull it off, I say, "Glory be!" I have seen too many congregations ready to pull the plug, however, when the great new pastor's second year has not matched the first.

As one who cares about congregations, I have to say that overall this theory leads to a few great successes and a whole raft of disappointments. If this is the way to change congregations across the country, we will have to learn how to set up schools of charisma and turn out a whole lot more great leaders than I see around me. Suggesting such a strategy, of course, points to its absurdity, and I decided long ago that the enterprise was one I did not want to get involved in. I salute those with those gifts, and I try to learn from them. But I do not kid myself that I know how to cause such leaders to develop, and I despair of trying to see that they are matched to congregations who can support that style of leading.

The technological model is one I am personally often tempted to use. It assumes that the way through our divisions and differences about congregational life is to find the new technology that, if we learn it and use it, will lead us out of the wilderness. I refer to various concepts of visioning, strategic planning, demographic analysis, future searching, and so forth. There is a pretty large industry around that builds on the hopes of those seeking such an answer. Every year or two a new band of technologists shows up and publishes the "in" book about change. Each technologist in turn becomes the author of the newest best seller and the darling of the lecture circuit. Some of these talented people build empires of integrated publishing, conference leadership, and consulting.

I describe this phenomenon with some discomfort, because lots of people seem to think that is what I do! I must say I have learned from these genuinely bright, sometimes brilliant people and much of it has been very helpful. Some of the tools they sell actually fit certain situations and can work. In the final analysis, however, I have to say I find that although this model is often helpful, it does not lead many of us out of the woods, and the technologies do not fit many situations. And this kind of help can make you increasingly dependent upon the specialist who is selling it.

Which brings me to the dialogical team model, the third of the models. I see in congregations. This model assumes that change is the product of a group of people

- working together to discover what changes are occurring in the environment and what those changes demand in response,
- assessing and improving their own abilities to respond to or challenge the changes in their internal and external contexts,
- using the leadership of the people present and looking for new leadership resources wherever they can find them, and
- making the best decisions they can where they are.

This work is undramatic and tough. It takes a long time, and there are no guarantees of success. Leaders who work with this model have to figure out how they got where they are, what needs to change, how to overcome obstacles, and how to come together in working teams. In my experience this process is helped enormously by a spirit of dialogue in the congregation, often beginning with the development of genuine dialogue between the designated leader (often a clergyperson) and the current lay leaders.

Such a team does not come together easily or quickly. Denominational definitions and legal systems can sometimes be supportive but are often obstacles. When it works, the change can be spectacular. Ditto the reverse. It is no secret that this third model is the one I put my money on most of the time. Not that I denigrate the other two. But I think this model is within the realm of possibility for most of us, and—let me be honest—I think it best epitomizes the kind of leadership God is calling us to in a posthierarchical world.

Given these three models, how does a congregation choose the kind of leadership it needs and make the model work for its own situation?

It was in 1975 that some colleagues and I gathered in St. Louis to look at a new role for ordained clergy. By the end of the three- or four-day conference, we had begun to describe that role, and we had named it "intentional interim pastorate." None of us who were there realized we had hit on something big and important. I bring that up now because, without knowing it, I think we were exploring a kind of ministry that helps a congregation choose the model of ministry that suits it best. Interim ministry does so by encouraging and practicing the processes of dialogical leadership.

The interim pastorate is *not* a demonstration of the dialogical team model, but it is in many cases one way for a congregation to begin thinking and using the model. It can help a congregation—whatever its model of leadership, whatever its real and unreal expectations of future leadership, begin doing the things one must do to build dialogue in leadership.

Bill Avery, in this book, does not tell you how to do anything. He does not say, "One way is the only way." What he does is give you some detailed snapshots of congregations and their leaders trying to work their way through a crisis. The crisis is one that every congregation has from time to time and one your congregation will probably have within the next five years—the change of pastoral leadership. He points out what those dynamics are like, and he shows how one trained as an interim pastor can make a difference in the ensuing effectiveness of the congregation.

These are stories about how faithful congregations have attempted to build toward and discover a kind of leadership model that works for them. These are stories from which your congregation can learn much.

LOREN B. MEAD

Preface

Mainline Protestant denominations have discovered the value of bringing specially trained and gifted pastors into pastoral vacancies, especially after a congregational crisis severe enough that either the pastor or a significant number of members have left. An *intentional* interim minister has received special training and, by virtue of that training, differs from retired ministers or other clergy who may be assigned to parishes between pastors. In informal parlance, a minister who serves in this way is sometimes called simply an "interim," as is the interval between settled pastors.

I learned the value of interim ministers in the two parishes I served as pastor. In both congregations my predecessor had been asked to leave. In the first congregation, a wonderfully skilled retired pastor had served during the gap of more than two years, and I benefited greatly from the healing he had brought about. The second congregation had had no interim pastor of any kind, and I found myself working at some of the very tasks that intentional interims customarily attend to.

When I was called to be a seminary professor 19 years ago, I began to read Alban Institute founder Loren B. Mead's work on the key opportunities during pastoral transitions and his early writing on the benefits of intentional interim ministers. In the past 19 years, I have examined hundreds of congregations through the field-education program I direct at Gettysburg Seminary. I have seen repeatedly the accuracy of the statement that transitions between pastors are key times for change, and that intentional interim ministers bring healing with a skill that most untrained interims do not have. As a professor who teaches evangelism and brings passion to the subject of parish renewal, I sought out, for the research project upon which this book is based, congregations that had experienced revitalization through the work of intentional interim ministers, and chose to write about how these outcomes were accomplished.

Selecting the Study Sites

The Interim Ministry Network—a national, ecumenical accrediting agency headquartered in Bethesda, Maryland—offers training through classes and workshops for pastors who seek this special call. With one exception, it was through the Interim Ministry Network that I found the sites used in this book. All of the intentional interim ministers described belong to the network. I first learned the names of these intentional interims and then asked each to point me to a congregation where he or she had recently worked—one that I could use as a study site. Of course, the present pastor at each site and the congregational leaders also approved my use of their church for the study.

The process of finding the Baptist congregation in North Carolina differed. I had learned that the Southern Baptists in that state used intentional interims trained through the Center for Congregational Health, part of the North Carolina Baptist Hospital, School of Pastoral Care. This organization pointed me to the intentional interim who served Reasonable Baptist Church.

Intentional interims are not open to permanent calls at the congregations they serve. They come in to do a specific job between settled pastorates, and then they leave. Their task is to bring enough healing to a congregation that it is prepared to call an appropriate minister for a settled pastorate. Interims usually stay between one and two years in each congregation. In four of the six congregations I studied, the length of stay of the intentional interims averaged 18 months. A fifth stayed for two and a half years, but commented that the assignment was by far the longest of all 15 of her interim calls. The remaining intentional interim team stayed for three years but could have left after two years.

Research Methodology

From the intentional interim who had served each congregation, I received a brief report on the crisis in the church, the interim's intervention during the vacancy between pastors, and the subsequent ministry under a settled pastor. Then I contacted the present pastor at each site (in four of the sites that person was the settled minister; at two sites it was the interim minister). Each sought permission from congregational leaders to participate in the study and then sent me printed information about the congregations—

a church history (if there was one), annual reports, newsletters, church council reports, bulletins, correspondence, official letters of resignation, congregational studies, and other items. I also examined the demographic characteristics for the ZIP code in which each church is located, and sometimes neighboring ZIP codes as well. (Demographic reports describe population change, racial makeup, age characteristics, marital status, household structure, income levels, housing costs, educational levels, and occupational characteristics of the areas around each church.)

Then I visited each site to interview the staff and a cross section of congregational leaders. I used in-depth interviews with

1.   the intentional interim minister,
2.   the current ministers,
3.   the current staff,
4.   lay leaders during the transition and those in leadership positions as the interviews were conducted (about 20 individuals or couples at each site), and
5.   previous pastors and staff when I was afforded the opportunity.

These individual conferences (a few lay interviews were with a husband and wife together) allowed the people to tell the story of their congregation in their own words.

Extensive interviews provide a rich avenue for telling a congregation's story. In contrast to statistical data or analyses of churches gleaned by looking at objective facts, in-depth conversations go below the surface to unveil the heart of congregants' experience of death and resurrection in the parish they love. Throughout this book I have used direct quotations from the people themselves because they poured their hearts out about the happenings, past and present, in their congregations. In the interviews I saw all kinds of emotions from sorrow, tears, heartache, anger, regret, and bitterness, to joy, love, hope, and peace. I found great nourishment in the privilege of interviewing these saints of God. Underlying all their emotions, I saw people of faith committed to living as God's faithful servants, both individually and in congregation.

To conduct the in-depth interviews, I visited each site for a four- to five-day period between January and September 2001. I always interviewed over an extended weekend so that I could also participate in all weekend worship services, Sunday school, and other church events. Laypeople were also freer to converse with me on the weekends. I recorded every interview and had all of the audiotapes transcribed for my use in writing the book.

In all the interviews, I asked the same list of questions that focused on four areas: the crisis in the church, its history, the role and function of the intentional interim, and the leadership of the present settled pastor. Overlaying these areas were questions about the mission of the church, biblical themes, and evidence of or lack of pastoral leadership. I asked the intentional interims the same questions, but also devised a set of questions especially for them.

Who Should Read This Book

The primary audience for this book is any pastor or lay leader who wants to renew or revitalize his or her congregation. This book will be particularly helpful also to any pastor assuming a new call or appointment. In most cases, the new pastor will not have had the benefit of an intentional interim as predecessor, and so will have to do some of the healing work done by the interims portrayed in this book. Lay leaders at a church where a pastoral change is imminent will also find this research helpful as they lead their congregation through the pastoral vacancy period. Moreover, laity who have newly called a pastor, especially where some level of conflict continues in the congregation, can help their minister by examining this research, because the pastor will be facing many of the same issues described in this book.

I have more specialized audiences in mind for this book as well. Anyone who is contemplating a career as an intentional interim will find six wonderful examples of what that ministry entails. Judicatory officials who deal with pastoral transitions may find help from this book in understanding the role of the intentional interim and in deciding when one may or may not be needed. A book with living examples of how congregations can be turned around to venture in new missional directions will be eagerly sought by those who have to deal with vacancies every day. Finally, seminary students can benefit from this book. Since the majority of mainline Protestant churches in this country are discouraged and in decline, examples of congregations that have reversed this pattern will be cheering to students. It is also valuable to both pastors and seminarians to understand when they are issued a regular call, but follow a previous long pastorate, or inherit a great deal of unresolved conflict from the last pastorate, that they may in fact become unofficial and unintentional interim ministers.

Structure of This Book

In many books, the most important chapters are the first, which sets up the argument or hypothesis, and the conclusion, which states the results of the research. One reads the body of the book both to understand how the author came to her or his conclusions and to glean further information about the conclusions. Such is not the case in this book. More than a generation ago, Marshall McLuhan, the specialist in communication theory, helped change the way we view communication with his famous statement, "The medium is the message." Elaborating on this sentence, he contended that the medium (for example, radio, television, print) was just as important, and even more important, than the content of the message it carried. In a similar vein, I assert that the examples in this book are the primary message, and my conclusions from them are secondary. Therefore, I invite the reader to examine carefully the six case studies because they are the medium that unlocks the heart of this book.

While the story of each congregation is unique and the chapters do not contain exactly the same categories, all chapters will have the following features:

1. *Introduction and Crisis.* Each chapter begins with a snapshot of life during the crisis, vacancy, or rebirth. A description of the crisis that led to the calling of an intentional interim minister follows. In these sections one will learn why the dissension was so severe for the congregation.
2. *Historical Section.* The crisis developed out of a longer history that planted the seeds for the strife. This section will allow the reader to examine the longer-term and perhaps more deeply rooted issues that presented fertile ground for a crisis to develop.
3. *Intentional Interim Ministers.* The intervention of these specially trained pastors is examined both in terms of who they are and what they did. This section begins to show the gifts, adaptive mechanisms, and special training these leaders brought to begin healing the open wounds of the crisis.
4. *Settled Pastorate.* This section examines the way these pastors built on the healing begun by the interims and then began to emphasize the mission outside the church as well as the health within. Again, the ability of these leaders to adapt to the particular needs of the congregation is shown through what the pastors have been able to accomplish, without neglecting the issues still facing the church.

5. *Future*. Finally, each chapter ends with a brief section on the pitfalls and promises for the future of each congregation. In none of these congregations is a healthy, productive future guaranteed. The potential for faithful development versus the risk of stagnation and decline is appraised.

The final chapter of the book points out the significant conclusions that emerged from the research. The congregations are situated in different parts of the country, represent different denominations and polities, different sizes and ages, different cultures and theological orientations. Yet there are common conclusions to be drawn from these different settings. The important findings include the ability of congregations in severe crisis to reverse themselves, the key role of intentional interim ministers, the importance of the adaptability between pastors and congregations, and the importance of mission beyond the walls of the churches. However, most important in this book is the simple telling of each congregation's story, because we can best learn about the death and resurrection of churches by examining the actual stories of six congregations that have done exactly that.

Acknowledgments

Many people contributed to this book. First, the intentional interims pointed me to a congregation to study and provided rich material not only about the church whose transition they had led but also about the calling of intentional interim ministers. Second, the settled pastors obtained permission from their church leadership for me to study their church, set up my schedule of interviews, spent a lot of formal and informal time with me, and in most cases read the chapters I wrote about their church. While they may not have agreed with everything I wrote, they helped me get the factual information correct. I thank all of them.

I also thank the following people from the Gettysburg, Pennsylvania, area who contributed to the preparation of this book: Kelli Leonard, who transcribed every audiotape so I could deal with the interviews in printed form; Katie Deighan and Kathy Avery, who painstakingly read the manuscript for spelling, grammar, and unclear passages; Sara Mummert of the Gettysburg Lutheran Seminary Library staff, who helped to research the questions I threw her way; and especially Rob Blezard, who used his expertise as a writer and editor to improve my prose, tighten up and shorten my manuscript, and reframe somewhat the arrangement and argument in the introduction and conclusion. A warm thank-you also goes to the board of directors at Gettysburg Seminary, President Michael Cooper-White, and Dean Norma Wood, for their encouragement and support, and particularly for granting me a sabbatical to research and write this book.

At the Alban Institute, President James P. Wind and managing editor David Lott originally encouraged me to write a book on the theme "death and resurrection in churches." From the time I signed a contract to write this book, acquisitions editor Beth Gaede took over as my editor and not only suggested adding a Southern Baptist congregation but also helped guide my manuscript from beginning to end. Jean Caffey Lyles served as my copy editor. I gratefully thank all these Alban people.

Only a generous research grant from the Louisville Institute allowed me to conduct the research for this book. My profound thanks goes to the board of directors at Louisville and to its director, James Lewis. Finally, Loren B. Mead, founder of the Alban Institute, has been a pioneer in research on churches for more than a generation. All of us who are parish pastors or who teach parish ministry are indebted to his extraordinary insights. Because Mead is one of the pioneers lifting up the period of pastoral vacancy as a critical moment for change and hence advocating the use of intentional interims, I am doubly blessed by his willingness to write the foreword. Thanks, Loren.

Most of all, I want to acknowledge the constant support, encouragement, and help of my wife, Kathleen, my soul mate.

Rebirth
in Declining Congregations

This book will forever be coupled for me with the tragic events of
September 11, 2001. No one will forget the images and feelings—
massive death and destruction, horrible suffering, numbing shock, and intense
grief. But soon, even amid despair, the beginning signs of hope and promise
emerged. Hope came in story after story of people leading others to safety
out of the World Trade Center. Hope came in the courage of the New York
firefighters both before and after the collapse of the towers. Hope came in
learning of the bravery of passengers on United Flight 93 who forced the
commercial airline to crash into a field rather than into a strategic American
landmark. Hope came in finding a few people alive in the rubble. Hope
came in the knowledge of a suffering God who grieved with us on that day
but promised a brighter tomorrow—even victory over death.

On that fateful day, I had just finished my last research visit in the
Midwest and was driving to a small regional airport listening to National
Public Radio, when the program was interrupted by the news of a plane
that had crashed into the World Trade Center. For the next two and a half
days I watched and listened to the news constantly, first as I was stranded
in a motel and later as I was driving a rental car (that I had been lucky
enough to find) home to the East Coast. In the news I heard over and over
again about death and destruction, as well as calls for retaliation and
revenge. One newscast reported seeing the sign "Today we grieve;
tomorrow we avenge."

Thank God I also heard voices beginning to speak about hope, or
describing signs of rebirth and renewal. As I drove hour after hour listening
to the news, I realized again that the theme of death and resurrection stands
not only at the center of the Bible and Christianity, but also at the center of
life itself, as demonstrated by our best reactions to the tragedy—after death

comes not revenge but rebirth, new life. And, I thought, on a much smaller scale, about the book I was preparing that also explores the central theme of death and resurrection, as God has implanted that theme in all living creatures.

Some congregations are almost habitually in crisis, perpetually driving away their ministers and maintaining a balance of power between factions within the parish by continued fighting. Just as some marriages survive because the glue of the relationship seems to be in the continual arguments, fights, and bickerings between the spouses, so too are these churches glued together by constant fighting that maintains the fractious status quo. My experience with Protestant churches across the United States for more than three decades suggests that many of these parishes would rather die than change that pattern. In other words, there is no automatic guarantee that rebirth will *always* occur no matter how faithful, gifted, and skilled the leadership.

On the other hand, most congregations do not want to live in constant internal turmoil. Most members want the parish to be a "foretaste of the Kingdom to come." They want caring and mutual concern among the members and a sense of serving not only their own church family, but also others outside the church in the local community and in the wider world. When congregants want their church to be healthy and mission-focused, no matter how severe the current crisis, then there is hope, and it is at this precise moment that the possibility of revitalization exists.

However, conflict within a congregation does not usually resolve itself. Instead, conflict festers until the wound becomes infected, and infection contaminates anything in its path: the mission of the church, the sense of family in Christ, the work of the pastors, and the health and growth of the church. Therefore, the need for therapeutic intervention is paramount. The best time for this remedy is between settled pastors, and the ministers best equipped for this work are intentional interim ministers—professionals trained specifically to resolve bitter tensions, rekindle vision, and prepare the way for the next leader. However, intentional interims cannot complete the process of rebirth themselves, nor is that their ministry. They help resolve the crisis and allow people to turn from the conflict to the future by helping them discover their identity anew. For rebirth to occur, the subsequent permanent pastor must build on the foundation laid by the intentional interims and bring the renewal to fruition. This is the essential argument of this book.

At the heart of that argument is the theme of death and resurrection. All the congregations described in this book reveal such a pattern. All had declined into a period of crisis and even near-death. In every case but one, the crisis caused the congregations to pressure or force the pastor to leave. Conflict gridlocked the congregants and curtailed ministry to others. In each situation, intentional interim ministers were assigned to the congregation, usually by a denominational office. The intentional interims, using their special expertise, helped bring an end to the overt conflicts, heal some of the wounds, begin to prepare the congregation for the future, and equip the churches so that they could select a well-matched person as their next regularly settled pastor. In four of the six congregations we will study, the settled pastors built on the work of the intentional interims and revitalized the churches' mission.

Congregational Sites

As I observed in the preface, the core elements of this book—the argument about the role of leaders in establishing congregational well-being, and the death-resurrection theme—are carried by the stories of the six congregations I studied. While the colorful names of congregations, interims, and settled pastors are all pseudonyms, each case study is a real church with real people and not a composite. Here are the churches I examined:

Reasonable Baptist Church, North Carolina

The 88-year-old church is located in what had been a suburb that mushroomed during the 1950s and 1960s. New growth moved beyond the church's location after the 1960s. However, the whole metropolitan area has seen continued growth since the 1950s, and that rate of growth has increased over the past decade with no signs of abatement. Under the present pastor's leadership especially, the congregation has gone from a neighborhood church to a regional congregation, drawing members from a three-county area.

In the late 1980s, the church embarked on a large building-expansion program, and conflict between the senior pastor and the associate pastor started to play itself out in the congregation. Once the building was finished, the pressures of the factions supporting one or another of the pastors became untenable. Both the senior pastor and the associate left in 1992. An intentional interim served for the next 17 months with an agenda to clarify the congregation's identity, history, and purpose. Some members left, and the congregation began to revive.

The subsequently called settled pastor has built on the renewal begun by the intentional interim, and the congregation has grown dramatically in health and mission. In 1994, the average weekly worship attendance was 350; today it is 700. The fact that the pastor has been in this call for seven years gives us a longer trajectory to examine how, with health restored, a congregation can blossom in ministry.

Household Presbyterian Church, Texas

This 50-year-old congregation was built in the middle of one of the "neighborhoods" of this metropolitan city that developed after World War II. During the early years, the church added more than 100 people to its rolls each year. The church is buried in its neighborhood and is relatively difficult to find for anyone who does not know that area of the city. The character of the neighborhood changed in the early 1970s when the public schools were desegregated. Children from the area who had attended the elementary school immediately across the street from the church were bused to an integrated school. Parents with elementary school children began to move out of the neighborhood rapidly, and the area, which had already become largely saturated in terms of new housing, saw its population become much older. The congregation still has not picked up families with young school-age children.

The congregation dwindled in size and became elderly. Then, a pastor who was not well matched with the congregation was called, and the membership continued to dwindle and to become more elderly until some of the members thought it inevitable that the church would eventually be forced to close. By the time the intentional interim minister arrived in 1997, the congregation pictured itself as dying gracefully. During the interim's 18 months at the church, she helped the congregation believe in itself and its ministry to others and prepared the way for an appropriate settled pastor. The present pastor arrived in September 1998 and brought the congregation alive, brought in younger members, increased the neighborhood ministry, and made the members enthusiastic about the future of Household as a vibrant congregation.

Adrift Lutheran Church, East Coast

The congregation closed down an urban church site and became a mission congregation (without site or building) in 1956. The mission developer pastor served for 42 years, in which time weekly worship attendance grew to 1500. The church opened a youth center in the 1960s, was affiliated with the starting of eventually eight housing complexes (most of them for senior citizens), began a successful counseling center in the 1970s, and started many other projects that served the people in this metropolitan area. Population in the area around the church mushroomed in the 1960s and 1970s and now is stable, with the average home in the area costing about $250,000.

The congregation has experienced profound difficulties: the pastor retired, but remained in the community and tried to stay active in leadership at the church. The intentional interim, brought in from the Midwest, had finished more than 20 months just as the chapter was being written. This site is fascinating for our study because it has not visibly moved to a place of unity of purpose and mission, and the future is uncertain. Attendance at this congregation is now down to about 500 worshipers a week.

Established United Methodist Church, Heartland City, Midwest

The state conference of the United Methodist Church is a pioneer in that denomination for intentional interim ministry. At this site both a senior interim minister and an associate interim minister have been serving a three-year call extending from July 1999 to June 2002.

Established is the merger of two congregations whose buildings were both razed in a 1968 tornado that destroyed the business district of the county-seat town in this rural area of the midwestern state. The church has a million-dollar endowment, with almost all the income restricted, but at the same time it has had trouble meeting its budget. In the last 30 years the town has declined in population at almost the same rate at which the congregation has lost members. Turmoil came gradually rather than suddenly in this case.

Trouble came to a boil in 1996–1999. The congregation's members entered into severe conflict with the senior and associate pastors, and then with one another. A whole generation of younger families left the church.

When the research was conducted, the intentional interims had been in place for more than two years, and the congregation was seriously beginning to look at its future when these pastors would leave. As the senior interim said to me, "It is our intent that Established will discern a clear vision and enter into Christ-centered, mission-minded ministry with renewed vigor and enthusiasm for making disciples for Jesus Christ." The congregation now has an average weekly worship attendance of 240. Established UMC, like Adrift Lutheran, finds its future direction of ministry still somewhat unsettled until the congregation learns who its next pastor will be.

Majestic Episcopal Church, East Coast

This church has a distinguished history with prominent families in its membership, including a U.S. president and his wife. Mission at this congregation began to suffer during the latter part of a 15-year pastorate (1970–85). A devastating church fire at this time brought further hardship to the congregation. A subsequent pastorate (1986–1995) was a mismatch between the rector (pastor) and laity. By the time that clergy leader left in 1995, attendance had plummeted to fewer than 50 people per Sunday.

Reversal of the decline and the beginning of renewal came at the hands of an intentional interim rector. Says the present rector of the work of the interim, "He was the primary key to make the church alive again." The new rector had been in place three years at the time of the interviews. The church seemed to have been transforming itself in the past five years, and attendance at worship was approximately 100 people a week at the time of the research.

Peace Congregational Church, California

This congregation was the first integrated (multicultural, multiracial) church in its metropolitan area. The congregation also declared itself to be a pacifist church between World Wars I and II, had pacifist pastors and members, and fought against the internment of Japanese Americans during World War II. Today, it is "an open and affirming, just peace church of the United Church of Christ."

Under the leadership of the pastor, the congregation flourished from the 1920s to the 1960s. After the pastor retired in 1963, a long period of turmoil followed. Stability returned in the 1970s and 1980s, but a dysfunctional pastor in the early 1990s led the congregation to consider closing, merging with another congregation, or selling its church property. When the intentional interim minister arrived in 1996, the congregation was down to as few as 20 in worship per week. The intentional interim stayed for two and a half years, brought hope to the congregation, helped congregants believe in themselves and the unique ministry they provided, and prepared the way for a good match with the next pastor. By the time the interim left, worship attendance was up to 35 per Sunday. The present pastor had been at Peace for three years as this book was written. The new life and mission of the church can been seen in the growth of average worship attendance to about 80 a Sunday and rising.

The Importance of Pastoral Leadership

At least in the United States, pastoral leadership remains perhaps the key factor in the health of a congregation. This widely acknowledged dictum receives much support in this study. All of the sites described here had exceptionally gifted intentional interims and, in the four sites where I was able to trace the beginning journeys of the settled pastors, excellence continued with the interims' successors.

Of course, the issue of leadership is complex. Like great art, leadership is easier to appreciate than it is to define. What I disagree with is the assertion that only a minuscule percentage of ministers have the tools to be transformational leaders. I am particularly upset by the statement that only 5 percent of our pastors make truly effective mission developers and that the percentage of pastors who can transform congregations is even smaller. This assertion implies that the vast majority of pastors would necessarily fail. These claims seem suspiciously close to the "great men" (the sexist term is deliberate) theory of social Darwinism that was popular in this country in the latter half of the 19th century and was popularized especially by Andrew Carnegie in his famous article "The Gospel of Wealth." The theory holds that in the evolution of humans a few "men" have special qualities that make them always successful (men like Carnegie of course), whereas the rank-and-file population never can possess these extraordinary abilities.

Such claims are wrongheaded, but the church often acts as if it were convinced of the truth of social Darwinism. For example, a few years ago, a churchwide unit of the Evangelical Lutheran Church in America printed (for internal use) a document titled "Ideal Characteristics of the Mission Developer." Find the person who has all these characteristics, and one is guaranteed to have a successful mission developer. Never mind that faith commitment seems a footnote to the characteristics, no more important in the list than loyalty to the denomination. Never mind that these characteristics can be used equally well to find a manager of the local McDonald's or the CEO of a dress factory. The views are based on the premise that only a few have exceptional qualities that make them real leaders.

This book will help demonstrate that it is the ability to adapt both by pastors—intentional interims and settled pastors alike—and congregations that makes a good match and allows the examples of creative leadership that we will see. Of course, pastors differ in their potential for leadership. However, I'm convinced that genuine leaders have the ability to continue to adapt themselves to the changing needs of a situation. This factor is more important than having gifts and abilities that others don't possess. People wanting to function as leaders can develop the ability to adapt to changing circumstances.

Moreover, within the church, the capacity (open to all in Jesus Christ) to love others as God loves us is more important than any other characteristic. I am persuaded that it is not the superman or superwoman who is the best leader, but that leadership grows out of the relationship between the pastor and the congregation. As you read these chapters, notice how often in describing pastors who were unable to lead their congregations, interviewees said, "It was a match that should never have been made." Or, "It was a good match at first because the pastor's skills were needed for this particular ministry, but when that ministry was finished the congregation seemed to flounder." Not all effective intentional interim ministers would make equally effective settled pastors. Furthermore, as I got to know the pastors described in this book who followed the intentional interims—and they are wonderfully gifted leaders—I realized that if you put the pastors in one of the other congregations, their leadership probably would not have been nearly as fruitful. Again, the relationship between leader and congregation is most important.

Precisely because the match is so important, I think we learn best through lively examples of congregations where a good match has been made. We simply don't learn that much by reading a book titled *How to Be a Pastor Who Revitalizes Churches*, or *How to Be a Successful Pastor of a Growing Congregation*. Apart from the theological issue of whether we are called to be successful, the practical reality is that such books have limited value. Otherwise, we could simply post on a Web site a five-page paper titled "Characteristics of a Good Pastoral Leader," and our work would be finished. An intentional interim in this book had it right when he said that you have to deal with each congregation case-by-case, because each situation is unique. This does not mean there are no principles to be followed. We will discover some of these as the stories of these congregations unfold. But it does mean that at the heart of faithful leadership is a match—a bond between pastor and congregation—that makes quality, faithful leadership possible.

Biblical Images for the Congregation in Conflict

When the pastor-congregation match is not compatible, conflict inevitably arises. In my efforts to understand the conflicts the six study congregation had experienced I asked them to name a biblical image that would describe their congregation in the transition from crisis to beginning health. Several delighted me by answering, "death and resurrection." One pastor answered by referring to the story of Jesus' raising of the 12-year-old daughter of one of the leaders of a synagogue (Mark 5:21-43). He said he mentioned this passage because the church he served had become old and had some baggage. "The congregation hit a place where something died within it. During the interim, there had been a raising of something brand new, and you don't know where it is going, just as it is with a child. There is a lot of promise here."

Others compared their church situation to the book of Job, complete with all the suffering Job endured and the return of health and well-being at the end. Another likened the trouble in the congregations to the wandering in the wilderness under Moses during the exodus from Egypt. Two interviewees even made the further comparison that just as during the exodus the Israelites wanted to turn back to the fleshpots of Egypt, so some members wanted instant solutions and a new settled pastor who would make everything right, without their having to go through the painful struggle during the interim.

One congregant compared the dissension in her congregation to the conflict with the widows not being served in the book of Acts, an incident that led to the appointment of the deacons. Another likened her church, in its period of conflict, with the Tower of Babel, where no one understood the other, and the moving beyond dissension as a Pentecost experience, where members could hear and understand one another. Yet another talked about the Mary and Martha story, in which Martha felt neglected by Mary when she was left to do all the housework. Two interviewees (from different churches) pointed to specific passages that suggested one should always trust in the Lord: Proverbs 3:5-6, "Trust in the LORD with all your heart, and do not rely on your own insight. In all your ways acknowledge him, and he will make straight your paths"; and Romans 8:28, "We know that all things work together for good for those who love God."

Some of the biblical examples offered were not quite as clear to me as to their implications. One likened the conflict in his congregation to Solomon's wise suggestion that a baby be cut in half to determine which of two women was its true mother. Was the interviewee suggesting that both sides in the strife claimed to be "right" and the intentional interim or pastor had to have the skill of Solomon to solve the problem and move beyond the dissension? Another said, "A voice crying in the wilderness, 'let my people go.'" Was this simply a plea that the conflict be over or did this person mean to suggest that prior to the intentional interim the congregation was in captivity and unable to be itself?

Finally, the most frequent response to the question of biblical themes was a nonanswer: "I can't think of one;" "I don't know;" or "Not that I can think of." One person candidly said, "I am a biblical illiterate." I admit that the question about biblical images for their congregations in turmoil was not an easy one to answer on the spot, and I appreciate those who had either thought about biblical parallels before or who were well enough grounded in the Bible that appropriate images or passages came to them. For those who identified a biblical theme, almost universally it characterized a congregation recently or currently in great pain but now delivered or soon to be.

Life Cycle of a Congregation

Understanding the life cycle of a congregation will also serve as ideal background for this book. While the life cycle has been described in various places, I think that Alice Mann in her book *Can Our Church Live?* (Bethesda: Alban Institute, 1999), pages 1–12, describes it as succinctly and as well as anyone. Mann portrays the distinct stages of the life cycle as a developmental arc (bell-shaped curve) with these points: birth, formation, stability, decline, and death (see figure below). That is, social organisms, including congregations, manifest similar patterns of emergence and decline as do biological organisms—we age and eventually die. However, just as human beings recover from illness, so also social organisms can often be healed with intervention. This mediation can be mild (an antibiotic), moderate (angioplasty), or severe (experimental treatment for cancer). In social organisms like churches, Mann calls these levels of intervention ongoing renewal, revitalization, and redevelopment. She has put these factors together into a figure that helps us visualize what she means.

Renewal, Revitalization, Redevelopment

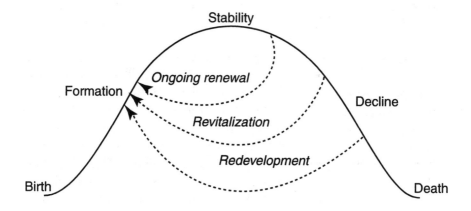

The Word "Revitalization"

Each of the six churches examined in this book illustrates revitalization. First, each congregation requires far more drastic change than that required by ongoing renewal. Renewal usually blossoms when a new pastor enters a congregation that has not been in crisis or whose previous pastor had not been there forever. Moreover, ongoing renewal can and often does take place during the course of a pastor's tenure. On the other hand, the six congregational stories in this book are not cases of drastic redevelopment. Redevelopment is what occurs, for example, when a struggling, declining urban German congregation chooses to acknowledge changes in its own neighborhood and to become predominantly African American in outlook and culture. Mission is redefined. Leadership posts and decisions are quickly turned over to those who live near the church. Revitalization, rather, is that middle level of change described six times in this book. It is the kind needed by almost half of all mainline Protestant congregations.

A Kairos Moment

Revitalization can take place in response to many factors in a congregation's life. But for 30 years, since the pioneering work of William A. Yon, author of *Prime Time for Renewal* (Bethesda: Alban Institute, 1977), Loren B. Mead, author of *Critical Moment of Ministry: A Change of Pastors* (Bethesda: Alban Institute, 1986), and others, the dynamic that occurs in congregations with a change of pastors has been seen as a crucial moment in churches' lives. Because a change of pastors causes congregations to re-examine their identity, the event produces a *kairos* moment when churches may be more open to change than during a settled pastorate. Hence, new and exciting paths of ministry can be considered and begun. This book will address new mission directions begun during and after an interim. When I use the word "mission," I mean it in the broadest sense. Faithful congregations focus not inward, but outward—toward their community, the wider church, and the needs of the world. Mission includes evangelism but is not exclusively evangelism. Like Jesus' ministry, mission means being involved in helping the neighbor in need, physically and emotionally as well as spiritually.

Just as the interim is a *kairos* moment in that it offers opportunity for refocusing mission, it also gives congregations a chance to heal from old wounds. The frequent need for significant healing and change during the vacancy between settled pastorates is obvious to any student of the American religious scene. Let me use as an example the results of an exhaustive study of ELCA congregations (my own denomination) done in the mid-1990s and reported in a booklet called *A Profile: Facts About the Congregations of the Evangelical Lutheran Church in America.* That study reported that within the past five years, 42 percent of ELCA congregations had experienced conflict leading to the resignation of the pastor or the departure of a significant portion of the congregation. Further, according to the study, about 55 percent of these conflicts involved pastoral leadership. In conflictual situations, the issue most often cited was whether the minister was providing appropriate leadership. Moreover, only a third of the churches reported that disagreements and conflicts were dealt with openly and were understood as a natural part of the congregation's life and growth. Only 24 percent reported that they had a definite shared vision, 26 percent indicated a fairly widely held shared vision, and a whopping 50 percent reported little or no shared vision. It is no wonder that 39 percent of the congregations in this study were losing members in a growing community! I think these figures are typical for mainline Protestant denominations.

The risk of crisis increases every time a change of pastors occurs. Every leader has detractors who can foment division by demanding that any new pastor please them more than the predecessor did. Members who were comfortable with the departing minister may be threatened if a new pastor is different from the predecessor. Members who had long thought about leaving the church use the vacancy as an opportunity to leave. Others simply stop attending. A change of pastors usually brings a change in lay leadership. In fact, one of the tasks of intentional interims is to put new leaders in place. Power brokers with the previous pastor lose their favored position as new leaders are moved into key positions. Some former leaders accept the change gracefully and even welcome it, while others may be threatened by their diminished role and cause trouble. Other leaders under the previous pastor simply quit, leaving the congregation with a leadership vacuum when trained leaders are not equipped to replace them. Although any change in pastors creates the risk of a crisis, the risk increases exponentially when the departing pastor had been at the church more than 15 years or when that pastor left as the result of misconduct. Therefore, many vacancies mandate crisis intervention.

Congregational Size

Another important factor that will help readers make use of the six stories in this book is that of the congregation's size. The size of the church also affects the dynamics between pastor and congregation, and churches of different sizes need different leadership styles. Arlin J. Rothauge taught this lesson in his little booklet *Sizing Up a Congregation* (New York: Episcopal Church Center, n.d.). From an informal perspective, I might describe the six congregations in this study as three smaller congregations (average worship attendance about 100) and three larger congregations (average Sunday worship attendance from 250 to 700). From Rothauge's more refined perspective, the three smaller congregations are all "pastoral" churches, meaning they function something like a wagon wheel with the pastor being the hub, and everything that happens in that church radiates from the pastor. In fact, in these three congregations, we will discover that the pastor is pretty much the center of all activity and that little happens without the pastor's involvement.

The United Methodist church I describe in this book is what Rothauge calls a "program" church, meaning a church too large for a pastor to be involved in everything, but where many different groups and programs are offered. These groups, committees, classes, choirs are the loci of intimacy for people in a congregation of that size.

The two largest churches in our study are what Rothauge calls "corporate" churches. With such a large (over 350 in weekly worship attendance) membership, the senior pastor has to function as a kind of CEO. Indeed, we notice that the current senior pastor at the Baptist church and the intentional interim at the Lutheran church needed to have very well-honed skills in administration. In fact, in both of the largest churches it was obvious to me that the lay president or lay leader also needed good administrative skills.

While size dictates different leadership styles, the common characteristic of these leaders is the ability to adapt to the particular needs of the congregation they serve, including size. Finally, we should note that every church studied in this book is larger than the average Protestant church in this country since in the average Protestant church only 75 people worship each week.

Using Your Imagination

As you read the stories of revitalization in the chapters that follow, imagine how the changes described in these six congregations apply to your situation. If you are a pastor coming to a new call, ask yourself: How much of the interim work has been accomplished prior to my arrival? How much interim work will I need to do before this congregation can coalesce for mission? If you are a pastor in a settled call, ask: How can these six examples modify my leadership style for renewal of the parish? If you are a denominational official, consider: What do these examples suggest for the way I treat pastoral vacancies and the use of trained interim ministers? If you are a congregational leader, especially one facing a change in pastors, discuss with other leaders: How can this book inform the way we approach the coming transition? I am convinced that all pastors and congregational leaders can benefit from reading this book.

Chapter 1

Reasonable Baptist Church
North Carolina

"When the intentional interim came here, I thought it was stupid. Now, I feel it's the best thing that ever happened to this church." This comment came from the head secretary at Reasonable Baptist Church in North Carolina, whose 19 years in her position gave her an intimate knowledge of the inner workings of the congregation. A church member described the importance of the intentional interim, the Rev. Dr. Charles Goodhart, in this way: "When Dr. Goodhart arrived, we could no longer focus on where we were going. We tried, but we were not clear on that. We lost our vision. We couldn't have gone with a permanent minister. We needed Dr. Goodhart to explore with us and help us decide where we needed to go." What crisis brought an intentional interim minister to Reasonable?

The Crisis

On the surface, the crisis arose from a theological and personality conflict between the senior pastor, the Rev. Dr. Paul Mensa, and the youth pastor, the Rev. George Young. Members of Reasonable Baptist had chosen sides and were not talking to one another. Indeed, everyone to whom I spoke acknowledged the tension between the two. George had been on staff for 14 years and actually had more seniority than Dr. Mensa, who came four years later. Interestingly, while everyone I interviewed referred to George as the youth pastor, he had actually held the title of associate pastor for all but the first two years of his ministry in the congregation. George developed a loyal following among younger members, especially the youth and parents with children. Having served as associate pastor for so many years, he was ready to become the senior pastor. Some interviewees suggested that George thought he would become the senior pastor when Dr. Mensa retired.

The senior pastor had been called because of his gifts in administration—especially in leading congregations through building programs. "When Dr. Mensa came here, we were in bad need of renovating our church plant," one member explained. "We were doing mission work to the point of letting our buildings deteriorate. We could not maintain our buildings, and the state almost closed our day-care and nursery program. Dr. Mensa had a good reputation in dealing with the administrative structure of the church and was excellent at capital campaigns. He did a good job of that. Once that project was finished, it's almost like it was time for that pastor to leave. His mission was completed." That is, when the buildings were repaired and a new educational complex built, people thought that with the new facilities the church would grow, and that did not happen. Instead, attendance at worship and membership continued to hemorrhage slowly.

Members described Dr. Mensa as a sincere person and compassionate in hospital visits with the dying and troubled. However he was formal, known as Dr. Mensa, and could seem distant and aloof to those who saw him only on Sundays. He was older, near retirement age, while George was a generation younger. However, the two pastors had difficulty in communicating with one another, and the tension became obvious to the congregation.

For example, according to one member, George wanted to preach when Dr. Mensa was away from the church, but Dr. Mensa didn't want that to happen. The reluctance to have George preach may point to the theological differences between the two. This congregation had always been a member of the Southern Baptist Convention (SBC), but when the SBC turned ultraconservative in the late 1980s, Dr. Mensa led the congregation in a more moderate direction. Indeed, pastors and members were unanimous that this congregation had always been a "moderate" Southern Baptist congregation. Under Dr. Mensa's leadership, the congregation stopped sending delegates to the SBC in 1990, and the congregation became a charter member of the Cooperative Baptist Fellowship (CBF), a moderate group of Baptist churches that had formerly supported the SBC wholeheartedly. Because of a strong congregational polity in the Baptist tradition, Baptists churches could belong both to the SBC and the CBF. At the time of my research, Reasonable Baptist gave nearly all its missions funds through the CBF rather than the SBC. According to members, George was more conservative theologically than Dr. Mensa.

The illness of the senior pastor brought the tension, and the choosing of sides brought it out into the open. Dr. Mensa became highly allergic to fibers in the rug, paint, and other materials in the church environment. First, he moved his office to the second floor, but very quickly moved his office home, and eventually could not be in the church for more than an hour at a time. The communication to the congregation about this situation was not adequate, and many members felt he just wasn't there. Because Dr. Mensa seemed to some to be inaccessible, members turned to George. Soon, conflicts and divisions arose, with people supporting one pastor or the other and not talking to each other. Small factions huddled here and there. Dr. Mensa's backers accused George's followers of trying to drive Dr. Mensa away. Several members said the conflict split the church down the middle and made it feel as if they were two churches.

The conflict became so painful for Dr. Mensa that during service one Sunday morning he announced he was leaving. But after the service and later via telephone, so many people pleaded with him not to resign that he rescinded his resignation that evening. After several more months, George left for a call in another state. One month after George was gone, in June 1992, Dr. Mensa retired. That left the congregation, as one member put it, "without a senior pastor and a youth pastor and [with] members of the congregation in intense conflict with one another."

Background

Reasonable Baptist Church dates from 1913 when a group of Baptists moved to this rural community, located between the city and the ocean. As the area around the church grew, the congregation grew with it. According to the author of a history of the congregation, during the 1950s, '60s and '70s the area's population mushroomed, as did the congregation, with a net gain of 62 members a year throughout those three decades. By 1975–76, the congregation reached its peak membership of 1,710. By then, the area around the congregation was largely saturated for new housing. Not only did Reasonable Baptist reach a plateau in size, but membership also decreased somewhat from the mid-'70s until the new senior pastor arrived in 1994. In fact, writing in 1988, the author of the congregational history said that Reasonable "may have already witnessed her 'best years' in terms of numerical growth and membership statistics."

As the congregation grew in numbers, so did the size of the professional staff. In 1992 there were four full-time ministers: senior pastor, associate (youth) pastor, minister of education and administrator, and minister of music. There were two full-time secretaries, a custodial staff, and many volunteers. In other words, even during its turmoil, this congregation's worship and Sunday school attendance were large—in the top 2 percent of all Protestant churches in the United States.

After George resigned and Dr. Mensa retired in 1992, Charles Goodhart, the intentional interim minister, served from September 1992 until January 1994. In 1994 a new senior pastor, the Rev. Michael Excel, was called. He began his duties in August. For 1994, the average Sunday worship attendance rebounded to 419, and the Sunday school, still strong in the South, averaged about 400 children, youth, and adults a week. Enough healing had taken place, because of the prayers and hard work of the members and the intentional interim, that 46 new members were received during that year. The question is, "What happened between the summer of 1992 and 1994 that enabled growth to occur by the latter date?"

The Intentional Interim and Reconciliation

It wasn't that Reasonable had not tried to reconcile its conflict before the interim came. As one key lay leader put it, "The congregation came at odds because there was a split between the two pastors. Key leaders were drawn together, and we interviewed members of the congregation and staff people to get to the root of the problem. Neither side would apologize, and they both needed to! We tried to get them to talk and resolve the problem, but the staff ended up leaving."

Because of the Dr. Mensa's work with the Cooperative Baptist Fellowship, he and some leaders of the congregation knew about the intentional interim ministry program as an avenue to conflict resolution. Dr. Mensa himself seems to have suggested that the church leaders go that route, and they decided to follow his advice. The selection of the intentional interim was put into the hands of the personnel committee, and they recommended Dr. Charles Goodhart. After he had met with the council, he was asked to come for at least one year.

While Goodhart brought specific gifts that were needed for healing to occur, the members of Reasonable were also impressed with the kind of person he was. "We needed a wise, old guy that had been around and seen about everything. He had a good temperament. Everyone really liked him. He had a wonderful personality." Said another: "He was very easy to talk to. He came with the down-home feeling so that you could just sit and share what you were feeling. He knew he had to get things out, no matter how it reflected on him." Another person saw a strong gift in understanding people: "He was a keen person in terms of understanding people dynamics. He was so personable. He and his wife were great. He instantly brought a disarming warmth. He understood the process of what the intentional interim is to do. He developed a system to force people to get into conversation, but kept the confidentiality. He made us clarify who we were as a church and where we wanted to be. So he brought out the conflict, and we talked about it and got over it to see where we, as a church, could go." Again and again, people interviewed described him as kind, wise, and grandfatherly.

Qualifications of the Intentional Interim

It is my conviction that it requires more than a powerful and pleasing personality to make an effective intentional interim. One needs special training beyond the theological degree and ordination. Charles Goodhart had spent more than a decade as the director of field ministries at a Baptist seminary. In that capacity he worked in and consulted with congregations looking for pastors. When ultraconservatives took control of the seminary, he knew he would be forced out. Having learned of the Interim Ministry Network, Dr. Goodhart began the network's basic training. He was in the midst of training when he began his first intentional interim position at Reasonable. Subsequently, he became an instructor for the Intentional Interim Ministry, Inc.

Charles Goodhart argues that the interim period is a process, not a program. Therefore, interim leaders and other pastors can learn basic principles and methods to be used in the interim, and from their training, they have a basic outline of what they want to accomplish. But they have to deal with each situation on a case-by-case basis, because specific tensions, traumas, conflicts, and divisions are unique to each setting. Therefore, Charles believes "how-to" books are of minimal help to interim ministers and congregations, because they cannot get to the core of what is required to be an intentional interim minister.

At Reasonable, Charles Goodhart helped calm the waters. As one member put it, he "brought peace. He brought the us and them together." Dr. Goodhart set three broad goals:

1. Reduce tensions: "If the conflict piece is still hot, it will override everything. The anxiety level is way up there, and you need to get that down first."
2. Assist the congregation in claiming its identity: "I have thought a great deal about interim times—you need to lead the church into an identity process."
3. Assist members in setting goals and thinking about the future in a way that also helps them think about the kind of pastor they want to call: "I went through a process with them to develop a mission statement."

Charles initially planned to use the deacons as the transition team, but this did not work out. He envisioned dividing the congregation up and training the deacons to lead the meetings. Instead, he encountered "one of the most demoralized group of deacons I have ever seen." This group was as angry and divided as was the congregation. "I feel there were too many of them [43–44 deacons] and that they had lost their influence with the congregation. They were shuffled into the corner. The group that should have been able to manage conflict because of their pastoral relationship to the members assigned to them was ineffective."

Instead of using deacons as the lead group, the interim organized a transition team of 25 members (including some deacons) and divided it into five subcommittees, one for each of the developmental tasks for interim churches: history, denominational ties, leadership, new identity, and commitment to new leadership. The congregation spent a little more than a year, largely in 1993, working intensely on the task of bringing the congregation together again. Hard work is an essential part of any healing process, and a large percentage of Reasonable's members was willing to give time, energy, and effort to address the emotional, spiritual, and theological upheavals so that healing could take place.

History Subcommittee. Dr. Goodhart invited the congregation to consider its own history and the current dissension. He told Reasonable's members they first had to get the hurts out and acknowledge them as real before any other step could be taken. To do so, he engaged in a process that the members found to be helpful and informative. First, the church organized around Wednesday night sharing sessions. Formal sessions were held in October and twice in November of 1992. At these sessions the members were divided into small groups, with a facilitator asking prepared questions. People were invited to talk freely about the conflict, about how they had been hurt, and about how they felt a pastor or pastors had been unfairly treated. The facilitator recorded the responses and submitted them in a written report to the subgroup. Deacons held cottage meetings with their deacon families (the congregation is divided up geographically into groups, and a deacon is assigned to each group). Deacon families were asked the same questions, and the deacons recorded these comments and passed them on to the subgroup. The members who participated in small groups committed themselves to keep confidential what was said in these meetings.

During early 1993, the history subgroup met many times to compile and group all the information obtained at the Wednesday night sharing sessions and deacon cottage meetings. Dr. Goodhart shared with the whole congregation many of the comments. Interviewees said the small-group work and the anonymous sharing of comments had a tremendous cleansing effect on the members. "He showed us how important each of us was to the church," one member said, "We had to communicate, and it gave a feeling of being valuable in the church. We began to appreciate what the people we had disagreed with were worth and how much they meant to the church. . . . When people can express our feelings without anger, there can be healing."

Second, on the occasion of a history banquet, in December 1992, long rolls of paper were hung on the walls of a long hallway in the parish hall. It formed a time line on which members were encouraged to write their piece of history at Reasonable. Members put down all kinds of items about their church life, from dates of baptisms, weddings, and deaths to significant congregational events, pastors coming and going, and world events. The time line helped them identify why this congregation meant so much to them and celebrate all the good times in the church. The time line also helped everyone see the extent of involvement of others (or their forebears) in the history. Some people were bold enough to put some of the hurts on the time line.

Reasonable also called more formal meetings about what it meant to be Baptist. Done in cooperation with the denominational relationship subcommittee, a regional Baptist official presented "How Baptists Came to Be" and "How Baptists Are Today." These formal programs were important to a congregation that had recently chosen not to be represented at Southern Baptist meetings and had affiliated with the CBF.

Denominational Relations Subcommittee. In addition to cosponsoring the two presentations, this committee met regularly and discussed the relationship of the congregation with the metropolitan Baptist association, the Baptist State Convention of North Carolina, the Southern Baptist Convention, and the Cooperative Baptist Fellowship. The subcommittee members met with past delegates to these association meetings and themselves attended all meetings after September 1992 when the subcommittee was formed.

The subcommittee was clear about its goal: "Our subcommittee has sought to determine the 'denominational identity' of our church; not to change that identity. In other words, we have sought to determine: Where does Reasonable Baptist stand in its relationship with other Baptists locally and elsewhere?"

The theological principle of their findings to answer the question is clear—freedom under the Holy Spirit:

> Baptists have historically been a diverse group of Christians each individually seeking the will and leadership of the Holy Spirit in their lives. . . . However different we may be, we also recognize that the Holy Spirit is calling each of us, man, woman, and child, to be all that we can be under His leadership, unrestricted by rules or policies or traditions of the church. . . . This doctrine is referred to as the Doctrine of the Priesthood of the Believer. We believe that such a doctrine can only survive in an atmosphere of *freedom* and *tolerance* and *love*."

The subgroup found its place in the Baptist world. "We recognize that in today's insistence on labels, our tolerance for the diversity of our members places us in the category of the 'Reasonables.'" The subgroup also said that this congregation was in favor of the CBF rather than the SBC, because "the SBC emphasis shifted totally from their historic main purpose of *Missions* to the purpose of *Theological Cleansing*, excluding all who disagreed." The committee stated that the church would continue its association with the state convention and the local area association, but expressed concern that the state convention may be moving in the direction of exclusivism. Finally, the subcommittee noted that the congregation had stopped using SBC Sunday school literature in 1992 because the denomination's literature "was driven mostly by the SBC controversy."

Leadership/Decision-making Subcommittee. The subcommittee studied information compiled by the history subcommittee and the deacons. It studied the constitution of the congregation and the constitutions of several other congregations with respect to leadership and how decisions were made. It met with the deacons, representatives of the personnel committee, and the leadership committee. At the end, the subcommittee identified a number of factors that had a substantial bearing on the way the congregation made decisions and how it was led.

For instance, the group noted the need for better communication: "Many of our membership felt the need to have more opportunities for input and more feedback from the leadership within our church." Second, they noted a lack of cohesion and coordination of effort among the many committees and, third, they acknowledged that there was confusion over the leadership role of the deacons. The subcommittee encouraged the congregation to find meaningful ways to empower the deacons and support them in their leadership roles. The deacons, in turn, would help to provide a means of maintaining communication between members and the pastor and staff. The subcommittee urged that a standing committee be formed to study the congregation's constitution and ensure that it remains a vital document defining how the church functions.

In regard to the polarization within the church staff, which then resulted in a polarization within the church family, the subcommittee noted progress during the interim period and saw the work of the transition committee as a positive element. The subcommittee compared its situation to a familiar Bible story:

> We found, at the conclusion [of the intensive interim self-examination], we had closed the gap and we were functioning well as an entire family, in unity. We believe God gave us this challenge for a very real and eternal purpose. As in Jacob's wrestling match with God, we had to deal with a challenge that tested our faith and our spiritual strength. We walked away, together, with the knowledge that God has blessed our efforts and restored our fellowship.

Without further elaboration, this subcommittee also concluded, "The problems we have experienced in the recent past are more perceived than real." I suspect that the group meant the love for the congregation and the underlying commitment were stronger than the divisions within the congregation.

New Identity Subcommittee. This subcommittee was formed because "When Dr. Mensa retired, Reasonable's identity changed. The subcommittee's responsibility was to assess that new identity. How did the congregation see itself, and was that view accurate?" The subcommittee assessed the identity of the congregation through *The Church Planning Inventory*, a self-study and congregational analysis (Hartford, Conn.: Hartford Seminary, Institute for Religion Research [formerly the Center for Social and Religious Research], n.d.) The group also collected census data for an analysis of the neighborhood. Finally, committee members looked at some community and social needs as possible ministries the church could address as part of a new identity.

More important than the specific findings of this subcommittee, however, was its shift of attention toward the future. Before this could happen, the hurts and tensions had been brought out into the open and examined. The congregation had studied structurally where it needed to change (for example, strengthening the deacon program for better communication; keeping the church constitution up to date). Now this committee could focus attention on the future. As Reasonable Baptist discovered for itself what it wanted, so it would guide the congregation in selecting a new senior pastor.

Let me offer a few examples of the results of *The Church Planning Inventory* from the subcommittee's report.

1.   Of the 14 core tasks of a church listed in this particular inventory only one, "Sharing the Gospel with the unchurched," rated high in "needed more emphasis." The congregation made this a priority in selecting the next pastor.
2.   While the people were generally happy with the worship service, they desired that a special part of the service be directed toward children. During the interim period the church initiated a children's sermon, and the present pastor, Michael, has maintained the practice.
3.   The people asked for more education and emphasis from the pulpit on stewardship, and immediately after the subcommittee completed its work, the congregation entered a month-long focus on stewardship.

4. The congregation asked for more local social involvement in the community, and as the report was written, Reasonable had participated in the blitz-build of a Habitat House. Over $5,000 was collected on a Sunday for that project.

The subcommittee concluded its report: "We believe this period of self-examination and evaluation has been very beneficial for Reasonable. We think great things are possible for Reasonable's future that will glorify God perhaps as we have never seen or imagined."

At the end of the intensive period, Charles offered his thanks:

The work was groundbreaking, and sometimes backbreaking. The members [of the task force] are probably unaware of the hours spent. I suspect, however, that their families are very much aware. Thank you, families, for sharing them for this vital work.

Also, a debt of gratitude is owed to the countless persons who cooperated with the process. Without the involvement of a large portion of the church, the work could not have succeeded.

Thank you for filling out the surveys. Thank you for engaging in the small group work.

Thank you for being patient when you wondered what in the world was happening. Thank you for being present when I taught principles of conflict management. Thank you for allowing the Holy Spirit to bring healing and hope.

Also, as the work of the transition committee and its four subcommittees was finishing, Dr. Goodhart announced that there was one more task and one more committee: "commitment to new leadership." This was a group to focus on what the congregation wanted in its next pastor. That is, given all that the congregation has discovered about itself during this interim, what particular gifts did it want to see in the new senior pastor? Intentional interims consider one mark of their effectiveness as the ability of the congregation to choose a new pastor appropriate to its situation.

The New Settled Pastorate

Charles Goodhart left at the end of January 1994 to allow the congregation to call its own pastor. Both the congregational leadership and Dr. Goodhart thought that the interval would be only a few months. The search committee did present a candidate with a recommendation that Reasonable Baptist call him. When he came to preach and engage in dialogue with the congregation before the vote, some of the final differences among people in the congregation came to the forefront. Rather than a personality issue, it was theological. During the open forum before the vote, the issue of inviting a homosexual to the church arose. The candidate talked about a homosexual friend of his and his desire that his friend be welcomed in the congregation. However, the homosexual issue produced a very tense meeting in which people disagreed strongly. The congregation voted the call, but because of the tension in that meeting and some other issues the candidate decided not to come.

Several people I interviewed said the problem was not the candidate, but that the meeting surfaced a key unresolved theological issue within the congregation. Speaking about the candidate, one interviewee said: "I think he had to go through that process. Someone had to go through that. His answers gave the dissenting folks at our church the chance to see maybe they were different theologically than the other parts of the congregation. After he chose not to come, several families, about 12, decided to go to other churches. They felt Reasonable was going one direction, and they weren't part of that direction." Eventually, the call committee came back with the recommendation of Michael Excel, who was called by unanimous vote and began his work with Reasonable in August 1994.

Michael was 35 years old when called as senior pastor. Lay leaders, when asked if he might have been considered too young to lead such a large church, indicated that they wanted a young person with a passion for mission. Moreover, all six final candidates were about the same age. Everyone interviewed referred to him simply as Michael—the way he preferred to be addressed. Because of his personal informality, using his first name seemed quite appropriate.

Raised in a nonchurchgoing family, Michael had a conversion experience at age 15. He attended a Southern Baptist congregation in the more liberal North. Thereafter, he began to participate in mission trips. After college, he turned to journalism and worked as associate editor of the news department of the SBC. At age 27, he decided to go to seminary and chose a nationally known Methodist seminary rather then a Baptist institution. He considered becoming a Methodist but realized that in his heart he was Baptist. Upon graduation, he accepted a call to a congregation of about 500 members. Reasonable Baptist sought him out. Happy in his first call, married, and with a four-year-old son and another child on the way, Michael hesitated to leave the congregation he was serving. Reluctantly, he opened himself up to the call to Reasonable, and in the end, because he saw great potential in the congregation, he accepted the call. The fact that Reasonable Baptist was interested in this pastor, who was far from the mold of the traditional SBC pastor, shows that what this congregation had declared about itself was true: it was and is a moderate Baptist congregation.

One layperson gave this cogent analysis of Michael's gifts:

> One thing Michael has done, better than any pastor I have seen, is to put into place a vision and a plan. The vision that we are all supposed to know is to show the love of Christ, live the great commandment. He has taken this approach and put it into place with some pretty definite planning. The church has generally adopted it and we are following it. . . . Michael understands the environment; he understands himself and this church; he knows how to approach people and approach problems. We expect way too much from a pastor. Michael does everything about as well as anyone I have ever known. He is truly spiritual and has a personal relationship with God. He is sensitive and willing to listen. He has a vision of where this church will be in 10 years. He wants to lead it there in such a way that it doesn't spoil what we have been. He is task-oriented, but not dictatorial. A leader has to be the head of the flock, but can only get so far ahead.

Several people I interviewed described Michael as a visionary. "He thinks outside the box, and yet he maintains contact with the box [the congregation and where it is]. He challenges the congregation to get outside the box." He is a skilled administrator with a knack for putting the right people in the right places. "When I think of Michael, I think of a juggler in a circus," said one member. "He gets a plate going in the air and keeps adding more and more plates and keeps them all going. . . . He is good at delegating. He gives people the power. When the job is delegated, it has been defined and he knows it will be done." On the one hand, he is described as "one of the most organized individuals I have ever seen. He gives us all of his personal goals and all of his goals as a pastor at the beginning of each year. He knows where he is going and where he wants to lead the church." On the other hand, several interviewees expressed views like this: "He is highly interpersonal. He is very feeling. Michael is not driven, and that is part of his gentle spirit. That is what makes him effective." So, he is described as having a caring heart, and likened to a warm teddy bear, ready with a hug and concern for each individual.

Wednesday Evening Life University: In his first year Michael both built on programs begun during the interim and established new missions. Wednesday evenings had traditionally been the occasion for prayer meetings. During the interim, Wednesday nights were times for meeting to deal with the crisis. In his first year, the congregation developed Life University, offering all kinds of courses—on finances, parenting, divorce, grief, and Bible studies. Michael used this foundation to restructure "the Wednesday evening study time to include courses that help us apply faith principles to issues of everyday life." For those who could come only during the day, Michael began a Tuesday *Lunch and Learn* study. Also, the Wednesday evening experience was strengthened by Wednesday family night suppers and by the Wednesday evening K.I.D.S. (Kids in Discipleship and Service) program (music, education, and mission). As a result, Wednesday evening became a key building block of the congregation's life together.

World Changers Initiative. Under this program, for many years youth and college students of Reasonable had gone to distant communities to repair houses for poor people. Under Michael's leadership, the congregation made this also a local effort. Each year, the congregation identified 20 or 30 families or organizations around the community who needed a new porch, a handicap ramp, a new roof, a paint job, new shutters, some yard work, etc. Several teams of church members periodically ventured into the community for home fix-up. In addition, Reasonable began, with other congregations, to work with Habitat for Humanity in local building projects.

Reasonable also started a yearly *Community Carnival*, a one-day event. The congregation invited local neighbors for food, games, and music, and began to assess needs for Bible study, parenting help, child care, senior adult care, and other shortages. "I am about mission ministry in the church and outside the church," Michael said. "What I try to teach is when you care for hurting people through Christ, the evangelistic part takes care of itself. If we all can do that, growth will be the last thing we have to worry about."

Although in his earlier pastorate Michael had not developed an alternative worship service, at Reasonable he quickly determined the need for a second Sunday morning worship service, before the Sunday school hour, and decided the new service should be "seeker-sensitive." Michael explained that it would stretch the people as a congregation, yet it would have the greatest potential for reaching the unchurched. Many long-term members were skeptical but allowed the pastor "the benefit of the doubt." For his part, Michael predicted it would be as large as the 11:00 service.

Michael and other staff planned for the new service with a Life University class of 25 to 40 members over six months, focusing on why people don't go to church. The class agreed a seeker service was needed and settled on a name: "The Open Door." The class held a trial service on a Sunday evening, and then took the idea to town forums for feedback. Finally, the concept was brought to the whole church. Many thought it was a good direction. Behind the scenes, there were questions: Would this make us two churches? Where will this take us in five years? And do we really want those types of people in the church? "There was skepticism in my age group about this," said one longtime member. "But now, I'd say that 50 percent of them go to that service." In the end the members voted to try the new service.

The Vision

During the first year Michael worked with the leadership of the congregation to develop a mission statement to be a guiding principle for "what our life together is all about." It reads:

> Reasonable Baptist Church provides a place where
> people experience God's life-changing love, mercy, and acceptance,
> and then together
> channel their resources and energies in creative ways
> to share God's love and forgiveness with others,
> meet human needs,
> and challenge and nurture believers
> to grow in understanding of and commitment to Jesus Christ.

"My style of leadership has been understanding that if a church does not have a shared vision, who we are by God's grace, then we will flounder," Michael explained. Even the new proposed Family Life Center, Michael believed, while it will be a rallying point, will not work to build the church by just adding bricks and mortar without realizing why the church exists. Interviewees agreed that the leadership core is well versed with the vision statement, and the majority of the members trust the leadership and know that Michael's basic vision is that Reasonable will reach the unchurched.

By the end of 1999 the congregation, under Michael's leadership, had adopted a concise document, *Turning Dreams into Deeds: A Strategic Plan for Ministry in the 21st Century*. The first page offered a revised mission statement: "Through God's power, building a community committed to Christ that lives the Great Commandment and fulfills the Great Commission." The next page describes the vision in greater detail but holds the length to one page. The third page describes the core values of this congregation: worship, Christian maturity, mission and evangelism, caring service, community, spiritual gifts and leadership, creativity, excellence, and Baptist heritage. The fourth page lists the strategic goals to carry out the core values. And finally the next 15 pages list and describe specific tactical goals and action plans for the congregation.

Also, Michael developed a course, "Life Is a Spiritual Adventure," that focuses on the process of spiritual growth. Four stages of the journey stand out: an exploring stage (seeker), an embracing stage (believer), an equipping stage (apprentice), and an engaging stage (servant). These stages are set in a mountain motif that Michael calls "The Servant's Walk." As part of the process, Reasonable developed a basic curriculum: Discovery 101 for identifying and integrating new members; Discovery 201 for maturing members, Discovery 301 for helping members discover and deploy their spiritual gifts and caregiving, and Discovery 401 for helping members share their faith.

An astute reader can see the influence of Rick Warren's book *The Purpose Driven Church* (Grand Rapids: Zondervan, 1995) and the leadership model of Bill Hybels's Willow Creek Community Church, near Chicago. Michael acknowledged these sources, saying that he and staff members had attended workshops by Bill Hybels, and he wanted more members to attend the workshops in the future.

The Staff

Michael took very seriously his objective to build a professional church staff. Of the two staff members who remained from the previous senior pastorate, one retired within a year and a half. The other, Clif, who came in 1991 as minister of music and worship, had remained neutral in the conflict between the senior and youth pastor. "He stood with the people during that time," according to Michael. "He became very pastoral after the two of them left. He has genuine compassion." As Michael developed his own team, Clif became an integral part of that team. Michael then hired Linda, a seminary-trained woman who came just as The Open Door started. She was selected because of her concern for missions and her expertise with small groups. Hired as minister of Christian education, she came from a similar position in New England. In contrast to Linda, Mark, a musician and composer of music who had been a youth minister for 10 years in another city, came into the congregation in 1995 as a layperson. Hired on a half-time basis, he became the first leader of the Praise Team, the name for the musicians for The Open Door, but also worked 20 hours a week outside the church recording children's music in preschool. He did this for two years while, unrelated to Mark's music, the congregation searched for someone to minister to seniors. Michael recognized Mark's special gifts for one-on-one relationships and asked him to consider ministry to seniors on an interim basis. Once in the position, Mark realized he loved visiting and conversing with seniors. As he was called to the full-time position as minister to senior adults, Mark stepped aside as leader of the Praise Team, although he continued as one of the musicians.

Troy, the newest full-time professional on the staff, was called as associate pastor for youth and family ministry 18 months before the interviews for this book were conducted. He had been youth pastor at a nontraditional SBC church, a seeker church. In accepting the new call, Troy entered a congregation that had a long historical tradition and had not lost its longtime members and yet had very contemporary elements like The Open Door and Life University classes. In his last call, Troy had received his Alcohol and Drug Abuse Counseling License. Michael sought out Troy "because he looks at ministry completely differently than the rest of us. We are trying to shift to his approach to ministry, needed for a congregation to move beyond the 700 weekly attendance plateau."

In its makeup, all staff members were in their early 40s, their ages within five or six years of one another (except Troy, who was in his mid-30s), and generally agreed theologically. Moreover, a sense of friendship prevailed (one interviewee mentioned approvingly that the staff was very "tight" with one another both professionally and personally). Some had children of the same ages. The staff and their spouses socialized outside the church. The staff met every Thursday morning, when staff members shared their prayer concerns and other ministry suggestions. No regular staff meetings had been held before Michael's arrival.

With the very competent staff, many other programs enriched the ministry of this congregation. Reasonable had a very well-developed Stephen Ministry program (under lay leadership, with each leader having at least 50 hours of training to minister with people with special and long-term needs). The 11 A.M. service was broadcast on television throughout the metropolitan area twice during the week. Members of the church went on mission trips every year all over the world. The church participated with 13 other congregations in an Interfaith Hospitality Network to provide housing for homeless families, assisting them in their search for shelter, jobs, and new beginnings. Members of Reasonable taught English as a second language at the church each week. These are examples, not an exhaustive list, and they point to the conclusion that this congregation had a lively time doing exciting ministry.

The health of this congregation was also evidenced in steady growth in Sunday worship and Sunday school attendance since Michael arrived.

Year	Sunday School	Worship	New Members
1994	398.7	418.8	46 new members 36 by letter of transfer 10 by baptism
1995	407.9	465	56 new members 42 by letter 14 by baptism
1996	426.2	522.9	71 new members 58 by letter 13 by baptism
1997	456.6	215.4 (Open Door) 412.0 (11 a.m.) 627.4 (Total)	78 new members 52 by letter 26 by baptism
1998	496	321.6 (Open Door) 353.7 (11 a.m.) 675.2 (Total)	75 new members 58 by letter 17 by baptisms
1999	479.3	340.5 (Open Door) 329.1 (11 a.m.) 669.6 (Total)	75 new members 51 by letter 24 by baptism
2000	454.6	349.4 (Open Door) 318.6 (11 a.m.) 688 (Total)	62 new members 34 by letter 28 by baptism
2001 (through October 2001)	467.5	377.6 (Open Door) 311.3 (11 a.m.) Total: (688.9)*	48 new members 33 by letter 15 by baptism

*(A larger number of congregants attend church in November and especially in December; thus-the average attendance for 2001 would have increased.)

The congregation delighted not only in increased attendance, but especially the sharp increase in new members by baptism since The Open Door was started.

Finally, this congregation worked to establish "small groups." Michael described the Life University as "our Wednesday evening series of small group studies." He understood, if the church were to grow larger, it would grow through a proliferation of small groups. I saw evidence of this phenomenon in an adult Sunday school class I sat in on. Part of the session was devoted to a discussion asking five to seven members to leave this class, which was growing too large, and to form another class. The leaders emphasized the need for the congregation to keep forming new small groups for the church to grow.

Most Pressing Issue

As the interviewees discussed the most pressing issue facing the congregation, three factors came into play. The first was paying off a large building debt Michael had inherited when he was called. This debt of over a million dollars was paid off in 1999. Meanwhile, by 1999 the annual budget had risen to almost $1.1 million. Second, the congregation had recently authorized the search for a new professional staff person, a minister of spiritual growth and single adults. There was some concern whether the church could afford another full-time professional, but once Michael made clear that he saw the position as vital to this ongoing mission, it was approved overwhelmingly. Several mentioned that bringing in this person addressed the most pressing issue for the congregation. By fall 2001, the new minister, Mike, had been hired.

Other members, however, said building a $3.25 million Family Life Center was the most pressing need. I found almost unanimous and enthusiastic support for the project. "Everyone has been dreaming and drawing plans for this for years," according to one staff person. Said another: "Everybody has ideas of what they want in there. . . . If it includes a working activity center for recreation, a walking track, classroom expansion, and so forth, it will really work." A layperson said, "Our most pressing need is space for growth. We are full in every room in every building. We need to build a family life center. We need additional meeting rooms, another kitchen, a bigger place for the youth."

During the summer of 2001, Michael, the leadership team, and lay leaders presented a long-range plan to the congregation in a brochure called *Building on the Dream—Reaching and Developing People for Christ*. The brochure provided details about the new Family Life Center—more classroom space for Sunday school and Life University, an institutional kitchen to serve larger gatherings of up to 500, a multipurpose room for banquets, concerts, dramas, and worship services (The Open Door and possibly a Saturday evening service geared toward generation Xers), a recreational space, including an indoor walking track, space for the Wilmington Interfaith Hospitality Network guests (homeless), including shower facilities, a student center, and more conference and meeting rooms for church and community. But the brochure went beyond describing the new building to outlining five phases of growth taking the congregation through 2007. The interviewees hoped the Family Life Center would be a magnet to attract people to church. One interviewee was very confident: "I don't know if we can handle the growth we are in for." It was obvious that many members have a high investment in what should be included in the new center. Michael, and with him much of the leadership, was determined that this center serve the community, not just congregational members.

The cost of the new building and other improvements was projected at $3.25 million—$2.95 million for new construction, parking and repairs on current facilities, and $295,000 as a "tithe" to missions for starting a new church, building concrete-block homes in Mexico, and other projects as opportunities arose. Reasonable was just beginning the public phase of the campaign—asking members for pledges—when the tragic events of September 11, 2001, unfolded. The uncertainties, coupled with the economic crunch, left the church well shy of its goal. As this chapter was being finished, it looked as if the total pledged might come to $2.3 million. According to Michael, Reasonable was "trying to think through the strategy of proceeding with the dreams without incurring debt. While the dream is not dead, it does appear delayed until better economic conditions prevail." Nevertheless, Michael noted that the mood of the members was upbeat.

Michael, the staff, and the lay leadership understood the importance of bringing on board the new staff person and building the Family Life Center. Yet when Michael, the staff, and certain key lay leaders talked about the most pressing need, they talked about the need for a shift to a new paradigm of church. Staff members described the congregation as having reached the 700 weekly attendance plateau. "Reasonable needs a model of ministry that does not rely so heavily on the pastor," according to one staff member. Said another: "We are at a 700 plateau. We have got to cross the hump of identity. We still have an issue of who we are and who we want to be. The issue of how big do we want to be needs to be faced. We understand our past and being a small church then. Changing some of the core people's attitudes is tough. They want the pastor to come visit if they are in the hospital. It is not enough if anyone else goes; they want the pastor."

"If I have to touch everybody, the church will be limited by my limitations," Michael said. "Are we going to be a church for ourselves, or will we be a church for the world?" Troy, the new minister to youth, was brought in because he had experience at a big church that lived out the paradigm Michael desired for this congregation. One mother of a 16-year-old noticed the difference, "Troy is building a team of leaders, rather than trying to lead everything himself. To recognize this new model is the next step to keep Reasonable growing."

Many lay leaders understood this issue. One long-term member identified the most pressing issue as "balancing the focus on outreach—reaching new members—and also meeting the needs of the old members. It isn't a conflict or problem, but our congregation is so missions-oriented now that there have been instances where some of the long-time members have felt too much of the energy is focused on that." However, this member added that overall the church had captured the vision that it was here to spread the gospel. Another lay leader understood that, while there was an underlying unity over the mission of the church, in some ways the congregation functioned as two or three churches: "The traditional church which tends to be the older folk, a caring and loving group that takes care of each other but wants less change, and the younger church that is less traditional and wants more change." This interviewee suggested that many coming to The Open Door—formerly unchurched single mothers, divorced men, and women with young children—were not really as mature in their faith and that their needs were very different. As in all the congregations studied, Reasonable's older members were the most generous givers, and they still gave a lot of leadership. "We need to bring up new people to fulfill the leadership positions. We have a pretty large group of people that are takers instead of givers. We need to change this group and bring them to the point that they are good stewards and willing to give to the church."

This phenomenon is common in church-growth literature. Congregations need to learn how to be a large church that does not depend on the senior pastor all the time, and that recognizes the need to develop lay leaders and helpers because the staff cannot do everything. The process is often described as changing from the mentality of being a farmer who is in contact with everything that happens on the farm to a rancher who depends on others for the primary daily care of the land and animals.

The Future

All members expressed optimism about the future, seeing continued growth in ministry to the community and growth in active membership at Reasonable. Clearly the concept of community had changed, especially in the last decade, from thinking of Reasonable as ministering to the neighborhood around the church to thinking of it as a regional congregation that drew members from three counties. Asked if anything could derail this direction, people acknowledged that the church could plateau at its present size, or Michael could leave and some of the staff follow, but clearly they did not think either of these was likely to occur.

Michael had thought about the future and specific goals of Reasonable more than anyone else interviewed.

> After talking with folks about what I envision, the future is having a tremendous network of small groups. These small groups will continue to meet on Sunday and Wednesday nights, but also will meet every night and day. Some of the groups will reach people who are unchurched—always the empty chair. Within a couple years, we will probably move to a two-tiered Sunday School, maybe having three services. We might have a traditional service to cater to seniors and a couple contemporary services that have different meanings. We would also have a Saturday night service to meet the needs of generation X. I would like to reach 1 percent of the population of this metropolitan area, or 1800 people in weekly worship.

One interviewee noted that at the heart of future ministry was the service to the community. She said that the congregation is a "heavy ministry church, with 15 to 25 ministries in the community going on." She said the members were catching the vision of going outside the church.

One long-term member said that 10 years ago Reasonable was reluctant about moving into anything new. "We have always been theologically grounded, but we didn't have the spirit to go out and reach other people. We were an inward congregation concerned with us, but we didn't go out. We are still cautious about that." But clearly this attitude was changing, and members knew the leadership wanted the church to focus on the mission to other people. The proposed Family Life Center was an example. Several interviewees said that they now had a much clearer vision of how this new building would serve their mission. "Our purpose before—in the 1980s— was the building project, but the feeling we have now is related more toward ministry and what we can do for the community, not for ourselves." Said another: "We are going to be a church reaching out into the community even more. Not just a church for ourselves, but for those that don't have a church in them now. We need to reach them. We need to make this building a symbol of the outreach. Somehow we need to reach out to every one; that is Michael's vision. I don't want to get the building done and have people say, 'Oh, this is for me, I'm not comfortable with others coming in.' We don't need turf wars, I don't think that will happen."

Finally, it is fitting to close by quoting a 77-year-old who was a 65-year member of the church. When asked where she thought Reasonable would be in the next five to 10 years, she said:

> I would like to see members going out and serving the community. The early members of the church were called Christians because they acted like Christ. I would like to see the members who go out in the community be looked at as Christians because of our reactions to the needs of the community and our daily lives. We need to continue to implement programs that help people in trouble. We have begun; we need to continue. The thing I do love about this church is that they are accepting of people in trouble and do not belittle them. . . . It is a caring church. Michael is leading us in that direction along with the help of all of our staff.

In order truly to serve others, one member suggested, the greatest need of the congregation was true dying to self—the everyday need of surrendering to God. "We want God to guide and lead us in how we can serve others and not just ourselves."

Chapter 2

Household Presbyterian Church

Texas

After becoming acquainted with Household Presbyterian Church, the intentional interim minister, the Rev. Pam Strong, quickly realized that one of her tasks was to snap its members out their sinking mindset. Because the congregation was made up primarily of older members, many believed it was in a downward spiral until the doors would close. On the one hand, Pam affirmed the members of this congregation, located in a metropolitan city in Texas, that Household was "the best kept secret in town." On the other hand, she was willing, as one interviewee put it, "to go against the grain and make people uncomfortable. She thinks that is what an interim needs to do." While people were divided about her forceful personality, many said she shook the members up and made them move on. "It was very good to have her here," one person said. "She opened the blinds. She made us define who we were. She told us from the moment she entered here that we were not a dying church. She planted that seed. She defended us." Pam functioned at Household not only to affirm the people, but also to shake them out of their lethargy. To understand this particular situation, we need to examine the history and crisis in this church.

Background

Unlike the other sites examined, Household was never a magnet church for the entire area. Household has always been a neighborhood church. In fact, it is so buried in a neighborhood that it's relatively hard to find and invisible to the larger city. The lack of visibility has affected the size and outlook of the congregation. Household began in 1952 as a mission outpost sponsored by two Presbyterian churches located near the heart of the city.

It grew rapidly along with the neighborhood in which it is embedded, gaining more than 100 people each year. Another mark of success: the church completed its plant, which is large, attractive, and serviceable, in three stages between 1956 and 1966. (There is still great love for the original pastor-developer [1952–67] by the several charter members who are still active at Household.) By the mid-1960s the congregation was large enough to have a full-time assistant minister.

One couple described the history this way: "This neighborhood was based mainly on people who, after World War II, moved here and started building houses here. There was a need for a church. The neighborhood was composed primarily of people starting their families and starting out in new business careers. As time went on, some of them became more affluent and moved further out or across town." Moreover, one decision by the city rapidly changed the composition of the area. The elementary school for the neighborhood is located immediately across the street from the church. In the early 1970s the city moved toward desegregation by busing children from Household's neighborhood to other schools in the city and busing students from other parts of the city to the nearby school. The neighborhood, which was predominantly white, changed very quickly as people with school-aged children moved out of the area. Instead of other people with children moving in, the population of the area became older as the existing residents aged and older people moved in. These changes were evidenced in Household as well. The congregation declined from over 700 active members to under 100 people in worship by the mid-1990s. Its large and active youth group evaporated. By 1990 Household was an elderly congregation, as evidenced by the 19 funerals Pam conducted during her one and a half years as interim.

On March 15, 1990, a devastating fire, causing almost two-thirds of a million dollars' damage, destroyed the middle section of Household's plant, putting the members into shock, and dislocating all groups that met in this part of the building. For a year, the congregation endured the smell of charred wood and the inconvenience of having sections of the church blocked off by plywood. Moreover, Household was between pastors at that time. When the Rev. Leonard Separate, direct from seminary, was called to the church as pastor in July 1990 as his first call, a few interviewees suggested that he might have been overwhelmed by having to cope with this crisis as soon as he arrived.

Eleven years later, when I conducted the interviews, members wanted to make two primary points about the fire. On the one hand, some interviewees said members united together behind the effort to make sure the plant was rebuilt. It drew them even closer together. On the other hand, some remembered great pain because of an incident that caused two active families to leave the church. A member entered a bid to rebuild after the fire. As his bid was not the lowest, the session (church council) chose another firm. The contractor, his family, and another family related to the contractor, all very involved at Household, left. This presented another crisis for Household, which had always prided itself on being family, on taking care of one another. The disruption was still painful at the time of my interviews.

Since October 1990, another congregation had worshiped in Household's church plant. The Presbyterian Church of South India used the chapel every Sunday at the same time that Household worshiped in the main sanctuary. Led by its own pastor, the South India congregation held services conducted in the immigrants' native tongue. Average worship attendance was between 50 and 65. Congregational membership drew primarily from outside the neighborhood, serving as a magnet for all South India immigrants in the metropolitan area who desired to worship in that particular tongue. The congregations related cordially, but fairly distantly. The congregations held one joint service a year on World Communion Sunday, followed by a fellowship hour. Formally, the South Indian congregation simply rented space from Household. While most members of Household remained content with the present relationship, a few members would have liked more mingling of the two congregations, perhaps even bringing the children together for Sunday school. The Church of South India had no plans to leave Household, so that their rental of space will probably continue for many years.

The Crisis

By the mid-1980s members at Household grew concerned about the future of their church and the need to attract younger members and children. The congregation had had only three senior pastors during its history until 1985. Before calling Leonard Separate in 1990, Household called a pastor, the Rev. Dan Younger, immediately out of seminary because they especially wanted to reach young people. While people really liked the young pastor, several interviewees felt he left them too soon (he stayed three and a half years [1985–89]). He had not stayed long enough to reverse the trend in the average age of membership or the declining attendance. Then the church called Leonard as their pastor, and the yoking was a mismatch from the beginning.

When Leonard was called to Household, he continued to maintain close ties with First Presbyterian in the city where he had earlier worked while a student. He was interested in political issues, locally and nationally, and worked in these areas at First. Household, worried about its own preservation, could not appreciate a minister who wanted to be involved in political issues rather than simply nurture the congregation. From the members' perspective, he never cared enough about Household Church, and he never severed his ties with First Presbyterian. Members claimed that he could seldom be found between Sundays and that he did not visit the hospitals, shut-ins, or members as frequently as they expected. Several interviewees said that he wasn't punctual. What really irritated them was that his sermons sometimes lasted 35 minutes or longer. Lengthy services grated especially on several members from the nearby Presbyterian Retirement Home, who needed to be back at the home by noon for the midday meal, and were often late. Two interviewees pointed out that while he was not a good fit for the congregation, he was a very fine man. "He was a delightful person, very warmhearted, but for some reason his dreams would never be realized here." We need to note, however, that although the congregation struggled because Leonard was not a good fit for them, it was already in trouble because of the age of the members before he came. In fact, one of the interviewees said that, before he even arrived, many members thought the church would be forced to close sometime in the future.

During Leonard's tenure (July 1990 to January 1997), attendance dwindled and some members chose not to come. "The church was stagnating under the previous pastor [Leonard]," as one member put it. "This church was scared to death that it was going to die. Everyone was so reluctant to face the future." Because throughout its history this congregation often had an interim pastor between regularly called ministers, it was natural for the members to heed the advice of the presbytery and hire an intentional interim minister at this point.

Intentional Interim Minister

As one interviewer put it, "Pam didn't please everyone." Nor was it her intent to do so. The situation when she entered as interim was the perception that, because of the large percentage of older members, Household was a dying church. The people were worried about not having youth. Many of the active members, however, were described by Pam as "survivors." They were loving people who had been around a long time. They remembered how the congregation used to be large, with many children, and they had been able to care for one another and for many others in the community. They were also in mourning because their fine musician had died of AIDS a year or so earlier.

As we have seen, Pam immediately offered hope for the future, by saying: "You are the best-kept secret in town." But she shook the members up and almost forced them to move from their nostalgia for the past:

> Pam was interesting. She came in and worked us very hard. She was very set in many of her ways. Many people had ties to former pastors, and Pam said to cut those ties, stop looking back, and move on. The former pastors aren't here anymore. She had us take a look at ourselves—what we were doing and what we should be doing. She prepared us for the coming of another minister.

Whereas Leonard was largely absent and so was not a pusher, Pam, according to the interviews I conducted, demanded a lot from the members. "She gave us a perspective on what we had as a congregation and where we could go," said one member. Another member described Pam as a one-person cleanup crew. She made the congregation define who it was, and "the disruption that she caused got this church going." Pam was willing to go against the grain and make people uncomfortable so the congregation might go through change and rebirth. Right away she emphasized that they needed to slow down and not rush in calling a new minister. She urged Household to take its time, learn what it really desired in its next minister and only then conduct a search.

Ordained in 1982, Pam Strong brought a lot of experience and expertise to this intentional interim ministry situation. She had earned a doctorate in educational psychology and had served both as a pastor on an Indian Reservation and as a professor. She also worked for a decade as pastor for a halfway house in the city, where she set up both psychotherapy and faith development programs. She became interested in interim work because she saw herself as having special skills in coming into a conflicted situation, ferreting out the causes, preparing for the next minister, and then leaving the congregation when it was time.

At Household, Pam designed and conducted her own "Listening Mission Study" to help in the transition. To do so, she set up a listening mission study committee of eight members from various groups or committees that make up the church. She also set up a separate listening team, of 25 core leaders in the congregation. The listening team conducted the interviews with the membership. Pam divided the congregation into four groups based on their ages as of June 1, 1997: baby busters (ages up through 32), baby boomers (ages 32 through 51), consumers (ages 52 through 69), and survivors (age 70 and up). The goal included everybody, and of the 177 people contacted, 114 people were interviewed.

An indication of the congregation's age is that 61 percent of those interviewed were survivors, while only 3.5 percent were "busters." Also 42 percent of those interviewed had been members for over 30 years. The questions Pam designed focused in five areas:

- Questions about memories of the church: What's most important for this congregation? What upsets you? What needs to stay the same? What needs to change?
- Questions about past ministers: What did you like best about their ministry? Least? What kind of minister do you want in the future?
- How do things happen in this church? How are they accomplished? How is communication kept open? How are things prevented from happening? And how is communication messed up?
- What one thing would you do in the coming year to improve this church?
- What will be happening in the church five years from now?

The report of the results of the Listening Mission Study is quite detailed. In each of the five areas, Pam described the marks of a healthy congregation and analyzed the responses by the generations in the church. The results were shared with the listening mission study committee, and the next evening with the pastoral nominating committee, which incorporated some of the insights into the church information form. Next, Household published key results in the newsletter, and, finally, on September 28, 1997, held a potluck lunch to discuss the study. The intergenerational event aired how the different age groups responded and suggested ways the study could be useful to the church now and in the future. Interviewees remember the time of the study and its conclusions and say that its biggest effect was to refocus the congregation from the past to the future.

Pam also brought organizational and computer skills that benefited staff and helped streamline office procedures. She also assisted the staff in reworking their job descriptions. Her secretary, Joyce, described her help with computers: "Pam did a lot to bring this church out of the Dark Ages." Intentional interims often update membership rolls, help organize procedures in the office, and occasionally bring computer skills to help office efficiency.

Pam arrived as intentional interim minister at Household early in 1997 and finished in the summer of 1998, when a call was issued to the Rev. Fiona Faith, who began her ministry on September 1, 1998. If a barometer of the salutary effect of the interim period is the choosing of a pastor who is well matched to lead the specific congregation, then this interim accomplished just what it was supposed to do. The congregation has blossomed under the leadership of Fiona.

Except for the leadership at Household, the work of the larger presbytery through the transition process had been mostly in the background. The presbytery had been helpful in suggesting intentional interims and letting the congregation select Pam. The presbytery also worked with Household to secure a new pastor. "They help us as much as we let them help us," one interviewee wisely put it. As it turned out, the organist/choir director and one other member of the search committee knew of Fiona's reputation (although they didn't know her personally) and thought she might be a good candidate for the church. With the presbytery's blessing, the search committee approached Fiona and eventually chose her as their pastor.

The Settled Pastorate

When I arrived at Household, a letter was waiting for me from an elder (a leader in the congregation) who had to be out of town over the days I was there. "I want to tell you everything great, wonderful, and exciting about Household," the letter said. "It's our pastor. The Rev. Dr. Fiona Faith is our queenpin, our sparkplug, and a superb minister. She is the nicest, most

caring, most enthusiastic Christian and the very best preacher I've known."
Everyone I talked to expressed similar enthusiasm for her.

A native of the South, Fiona Faith was an excellent student and avid
tennis player throughout school. She married her college sweetheart, but
soon after their son was born, her husband died a tragic death from cancer.
A widow in her mid-20s, she received a scholarship to earn a master of
divinity degree at Union Presbyterian Seminary in Richmond, Virginia, and
later earned her doctorate of ministry from Columbia Theological Seminary
in Decatur, Georgia. After serving as associate pastor of a congregation in
the Southeast, she moved to the city in Texas where Household is located
to become associate pastor of a large church there.

To understand Fiona's ministry at Household, we must examine the
potential she saw in this congregation that led her to accept the call. Fiona
experienced firsthand how Household was "the most caring and friendly
church in the city." Almost everyone described Household as "family," a
place where people care about one another and rush to help any member in
need. Members hastened to add that it is not a closed community but rather
inviting to visitors and strangers. When I asked a new member why the
congregation appealed to her, she immediately responded: "The real love
here." When I asked the secretary why she commuted almost an hour
each way to work at Household, she answered, "The congregation. The
people here are wonderful." Apparently Household has never suffered a
division that has split the church, although membership and participation
dwindled, especially under Leonard's leadership. Moreover, no pastor has
ever been asked to resign. One member said he knew God is love because
he experienced love at Household. One interviewee defined family in this
congregation as a loving group trying to do God's work in community.
Finally, one interviewee said while ministers come and go, the sense of
family endures. "We are very willing to add to the family," he said. "We are
not a closed group." Although it was an elderly congregation, Fiona believed
the profound level of caring among the members was more important than
their age.

Second, the congregation was ethnically diverse, and was open to
becoming even more so in the future. While the immediate neighborhood
around Household was predominantly white, the elementary school, located
directly across the street from the church told a different story. According
to a special report in the city's daily newspaper on March 11, 2001, this
particular school—an arts magnet school—had the following demographics:

African American, 43.4 percent; "Anglo" (Euro-American), 26.1 percent; Latin American, 21.6 percent; and Asian American, 8.9 percent. Fifty-one percent of the pupils came from low-income homes. With the approval of the congregation, Fiona and the organist/choir director moved immediately to reach these children by starting a children's choir. Also, Fiona served on the board of the after-school program, opened the church parking lot for school events and passed out brochures about the children's choir and the church to visitors to the school. While the congregation was predominantly Caucasian, it had several black members, including an elder, several Latino members, and a couple of members from India and China. The attitude of Household's members was captured by this comment from a charter member of the congregation: "There is a racial mixture in this church; you can tell with the children. That is a blessing here; all minorities are welcome."

Third, a renaissance was beginning in the neighborhood. The congregation was close to a well-known medical center that is the largest employer in the city. Developers and people who didn't want a long commute to work were discovering the area. One couple said their block (near the church) contained 22 homes and, a few years ago, very few children. In the last two to three years, many of these homes had gone on the market. "Younger families are moving in, and we have more young children than we have ever had. We love to hear the children out playing." In my walk around the neighborhood I saw places where people had bought a house for its land, torn down the older, smaller house, and built a new, larger house. I also saw a gated community one block from the church with townhouses selling for $250,000. On the Sunday I worshiped with the congregation, a couple in their late 20s—both young professionals—who had just bought one of the townhouses visited the church for the first time. (Later, I learned that they had joined Household.) As one interviewee said, the neighborhood was coming together and in the future it would become even more diverse.

Fourth, the congregation was running a small but successful program teaching English as a second language under the leadership of a member, with several other volunteers from the church. These volunteers worked primarily with Asian immigrants. Fiona supported and encouraged this program, and a few people had become a part of Household because of this program.

Fifth, the congregation had a very nice physical plant. Taking up the entire front of a city block in a residential neighborhood, the church building was long and thin with a sizable parking lot at the south end and considerable parking along the extended rear of the building. There was a larger United Methodist church immediately to the rear of Household, and the two churches cooperated by lending one another equipment for special events, opening up their respective parking lots for these events, and sharing their buildings to accommodate one another's overflow events.

Sixth, money has seldom been a major issue. One member said simply, "We have never hurt financially." Another said, "Household gives as much per capita as any other Presbyterian church around." In fact after Fiona had been called as pastor, Household launched a capital campaign to fix up all those little things that a building 35 to 45 years old needs: replacing rotting boards, updating the plumbing, releading stained glass windows, painting, landscaping, putting new doors to the sanctuary, erecting new interior lighting (including a bright light behind the stained-glass window of the sanctuary to be seen by people driving by at night), and installing exterior lighting to highlight the side walls of the sanctuary. The goal was to have pledged $250,000 by the 50th anniversary, September 2002. By March 2001, the congregation had pledged $251,000! Only one interviewee expressed concern about finances—that with so many of the large givers being elderly, what would happen when they died?

A sea change in attitude began among the members with Fiona's arrival. One person suggested that the people used to see Household's glass as half-empty and emptying. With Fiona as pastor, they now saw the glass as half-full and filling quickly. Another said that the hidden assumption when she arrived was that they were holding on until the doors closed, but when, two months later, seven people were received into membership on one Sunday, that assumption began to fade. From the time she arrived, Fiona emphasized evangelism, especially to bring younger people into the congregation.

When Fiona arrived, the congregation was down to three or four children active in church. The leadership wanted to close the nursery during church when Fiona came, but she pushed to have it continue, and since then the nursery has had as many as 12 children. The music program had long been a source of strength for Household, with one interviewee saying the choir and director were the one thread that held the church together after Leonard left. Fiona and the choir director established a children's choir by handing out flyers in the neighborhood, and by the time of my visit the choir boasted 12 youngsters, and was growing. In the summer, vacation Bible school was moved to evenings to accommodate the needs of the parents and teachers, with enhanced involvement of neighborhood children as a result.

To reach new families, the congregation had several times passed out leaflets about the church to neighborhood homes. Of course, Fiona not only championed this idea but also led each canvassing herself. Household improved permanent signage at the church and started putting out portable signs every weekend on the medians of the two main streets near the church to direct people to Household. Fiona had gotten Household listed in the biweekly newsletter for Medical Center employees. She had developed an attractive brochure about the church, featuring the stained-glass window that was now backlighted in the evening. Fiona's college-age son had developed an excellent Web page for the congregation that employed the same stained-glass window motif. The information on the Web page was updated at least once a week. Fiona also revamped the church newsletter.

When I was there, Fiona had just begun a young-adult group for people under 40 that had a mission emphasis and hosted social get-togethers but was not a Sunday school class. The congregation had monthly dinners—potluck or catered—to get to know new people and to catch up with each other. I attended a potluck dinner after church and was surprised to see how many people talked with visitors or people they did not know. An Encore group, made up of retired men and women, used precinct buses for day trips. (Government buses are free to go up to 120 miles on special excursions for six to eight hours for senior citizens.)

Good things continued to happen at Household simply because people were enthusiastic. "Our image is much better, and we are ready to invite people into the church," one member said. "When visitors come in the church," said another, "they leave thinking we are an extremely friendly church. Our congregation is in the habit of talking to them and making them feel welcome." I was warmly greeted by this congregation before the members had any idea of who I was. Of course, Fiona would like members to be even more intentional about inviting people to worship—including their co-workers, neighbors, and family.

Because of these efforts, attendance at worship increased from about 75 to 120 in two and a half years. Seventy new members were added, including more families with children and young adults without children. With the influx of children, there were now confirmation classes. Fiona added more special services, including Maundy Thursday and Good Friday, and gave them practical support. "She makes sure people have rides to and from church at night," said a member who sums up many good things: "The congregation seems more at peace with itself and its relationship with God. We were nervous that the church was dying, especially after the fire. The people now feel better about the church and the worship experience."

Household worships with a well-executed traditional liturgy using the 1990 *Presbyterian Hymnal* with a special "time with young disciples" and good music throughout. "The new hymnal is contemporary enough for us," one member said. During my stay, worship was upbeat and joyful, even without contemporary music, and with a strong sermon by a pastor who was not afraid to talk about sin (and to call it just that) and redemption. Special services offered a different fare. For example, on July 4 Household held a jazz communion service. Household was blessed by having a wonderful organist-choirmaster, who had also started a successful handbell choir. He has also written three books and recorded two compact discs. Shortly before my visit, he had been heavily courted by larger congregations, but stayed for three reasons: the warmth of the people, the fact that Presbyterian is the denomination of his heart, and, most important—Fiona! "Serving under her is indescribable. I think I'm where I'm supposed to be."

Here is how members described Fiona: "She is so down-to-earth and so vivacious. She takes an interest in everyone and everything. She is a motivator. She takes time to visit and talk to everyone." "She exudes genuine love and real knowledge. She is tremendous as a Bible reader and teacher. . . . Her pulpit sermons are exceptional and they come from the heart. Her pastoral care—I've never seen better in my life. She is very accessible. . . . She has suffered and understands when we suffer. She offers tremendous comfort and support. She is a sustaining part of the life of the church." Another described how she brings enthusiasm, caring, and a contagious, upbeat attitude to the church. Yet another noted that she has helped many members emotionally and has been with them through turmoil and illness. One interviewee noted her emotional balance: "She is at peace with God and with herself." A staff person said, "I can't imagine working under someone else. Her energy and enormous capacity to overlook someone's faults is amazing. I never have seen her door closed or never called that she didn't pick up or respond almost immediately." The only wish for a slight change anyone had about her was that she would be a little more willing to engage in an unpleasant confrontation when necessary.

Fiona described her leadership style as collegial—she tries to motivate people. As a teenager she played tennis competitively under a coach who became a phenomenal motivator by being positive and encouraging. Her favorite English teacher used the same methodology. Not surprisingly, Fiona is a dog lover. She said, "Dogs will do so much more if you praise and love them, rather than beat them down. I think people are the same way. You encourage people and thank them, and they respond."

The members concurred that she led in a collegial manner, and worked toward consensus decisions whenever possible. One member said she frequently asked, "What is it we are going to do?" She was described as "laid back" but not *laissez-faire*. "When she comes to a meeting, she has already laid the groundwork. She is a good manager." Another interviewee described her leadership style: "Fiona is not a hint dropper; she is very forthcoming. Her manner of presenting an idea might appear to be neutral, but it takes root. . . . She is very prepared, but she is not an authority figure. She is deeply respected. She does what she does through the grace of God, who lives in her."

Fiona empowered lay leadership to run with ideas, and she didn't have to have her fingers in every pie. Empowerment was a priority for Fiona, and it must continue or the congregation may hit the "glass ceiling" or "plateau" that congregations often reach when they have between 150 and 250 in worship. This occurs in large part because the pastor is the one who is connected to all the members. Pastors can sustain only so many relationships. Fiona must find lay leaders to take charge of ministries, or the congregation will be in trouble before long.

Moreover, while we note all the praise for Fiona, we need to remember the other side of this equation: The congregation went through hard work during the interim between settled pastors to get its act together, so the members had the self-confidence to seek a fine pastor and to attract someone like her. The excellent match between Household's needs for leadership and Fiona's gifts made the ministry flourish, thanks to the efforts of both pastor and congregation.

Surprisingly, none of the members could remember a mission statement for the congregation. Some said simply that the church didn't have one, while others vaguely remember working on a mission statement when they were looking for a new minister. In my conversations with Fiona, I sensed that developing a specific mission statement with measurable objectives was simply not one of her priorities. She was content to operate under a general mission thrust that she described as "proclaiming the good new of Jesus Christ, seeking to serve Christ by reaching out to others, and spreading evidence of God's love in the local community and around the world."

A review of the Web site confirmed this general mission statement. When the viewer went to the site, she or he was greeted by a welcome from Fiona that began, "Greetings from Household Presbyterian Church! We are a warm and friendly church family, and we would love to welcome you as a visitor or, even better, as an active member." This greeting went on to give a few specifics such as time of worship and directions to the church. When one went further by clicking on the tab, "General Information," one saw this message: "Everything at Household flows from the worship of God. Our worship seeks to glorify God through the proclamation of the word, the celebration of the sacraments, and through music and liturgy." Thus, only a hint of a mission statement appeared on the Web site. Household stands in contrast to several of the congregations in this book because little emphasis is placed on a defining mission statement.

One member, referring to Jesus' encounter with Mary and Martha (Luke 10:38-42), said that Household was a Mary church also becoming a Martha church under Fiona's leadership. In addition to English as a second language, the congregation was involved in several service projects, largely through the church's unit of Presbyterian Women and the choir, the two strongest groups in the church, and increasingly through the young-adult group, the "Seekers." Household was involved with the cancer center near them; Kidcare (a program that feeds hungry children); and Christian Community Service Center, a coalition of 40 churches with programs to help the needy find jobs, and to provide food, clothes, school supplies, and a Christmas toy store. The church conducted a food drive each month and supports the larger Presbyterian church not only with its benevolence money, but also through One Great Hour of Sharing and Joy Gift. Fiona involved adults in Habitat for Humanity and the children in the Heifer Project International, raising money for people around the world to feed themselves and become self-reliant. Fiona wanted to increase the involvement of the congregation in local service projects, as she could develop leadership to do so.

The Issues

When Fiona Faith arrived, the crisis had been whether the church would close its doors in a few years. The most visible need was to increase membership. To some degree that remained the presenting issue: attracting enough younger people so that when elderly members die, sufficient numbers remain for a viable, faithful congregation. "Membership. Yes, that is important to us right now," said the office manager—a volunteer position held by a long-time retiree. "While Pam was here, she had a funeral every month," he said. "It took a lot of our base away, and we are going to be losing more. We have to do something to bring more people into this church. . . . We are working from a solid base, but the elderly are dying off." Unfortunately, the office manager himself would die a few months later. Household especially needed children: "It takes youth to grow a church. Until we can get a youth program started, we aren't going places," said another member. "We may plod along, but we need youth in this church. We have lots of old people here." Actually, according to Fiona, there was a youth program, with a core group of about eight teenagers.

But as much as new members were needed, so were new leaders. "We need new blood in here," said an interviewee. In Fiona's first year at pastor, older, long-term members still largely held the leadership positions." One member doubted whether new members were able to take leadership roles. New members are either older (remember the Presbyterian retirement home is nearby) or young couples, both partners working full-time jobs and lacking the time (or unwilling to give the time) to assume leadership roles in the congregation. One interviewee worried that younger members would be overwhelmed in leadership. "The risk is burnout," he said, "because there seems to be a small pool to pull from to supply officers of the church." Since the time of my interviews with the members, the leadership issue has further changed in that many newer, younger members have been brought into key leadership positions. In the 2001 election of elders, all five newly elected elders were serving for the first time—one was in her 20s, and the oldest was in his 50s. Fiona herself recognized that it takes five or 10 younger members to make up for one older person in stewardship. Fiona defines the word stewardship as the use of time, talents, and money, and she recognized that she needed time to train new members about what stewardship meant for them personally. She wanted to teach giving as the fruit of gratitude for what God has done, rather than giving only to fund practical needs.

Future

The interviewees believed Household must continue on its current path—bringing in new and younger members, developing new leadership. "We have new people coming in," one member said, "If we can keep them, we need to keep that younger community growing. I see more of a transition in the next five to 10 years than in the past five to 10 years. There is going to be change, imposed by the death of older members." Fiona said the people were up for this change. While they were caring of one another, they were also open to change. More than the other congregations she had served, Fiona said, the people here were willing to work. "They don't expect their staff to do everything; they do things without grumbling. They take ministry tasks on themselves."

Because of the caring and commitment of the members of Household, one interviewee expressed optimism: "We are all in for the future. We are here for the long haul. We would love for Fiona to stay on and continue what she is doing, but it would not be the end of the world if she left. Maybe that is how we all grow. The Lord doesn't let us become too comfortable." However, most members thought their pastor was key to their future. One expressed it most succinctly: "I think the growth of this church will greatly depend on the minister. If Fiona stays, the sky is the limit. If she goes, I have no idea what will happen. Nobody has been loved like she is."

September 22, 2002, marks the 50th anniversary of the founding of Household. Fiona and the leadership of the congregation were already planning a gala event that would highlight the presence of the church in its neighborhood and invite the community to celebrate with them. Fiona was positive, energetic, and hopeful, and the congregation had certainly picked up these traits as they looked with eager anticipation for what the future would bring.

Chapter 3

Adrift Lutheran Church
East Coast

Mark Empower is a deliberate facilitator who has tried to encourage council and staff to take responsibility for leadership of the congregation. He doesn't control or direct. He lets the group squirm and find its own voice, to let them come up with their own answers and take control. His role is to help the church find itself.

The Rev. Mark Empower was serving as the intentional interim minister at Adrift Lutheran Church when this book's research was done. The member quoted above expressed most concisely what Mark tried to accomplish. It's critical to start out with this understanding about Mark's purpose and role because it was widely misunderstood in the congregation, and Adrift was divided over his ministry.

Adrift Lutheran was in a different condition in the fall of 2001 than most of the other sites we have studied. Adrift's turmoil had not subsided, and its future remained uncertain. A series of crises had left this congregation divided. Attendance was half of what it had been just a few years before, and people continued to leave for other churches—or at least no longer worshiped at Adrift. Some healing had taken place during the interim's tenure, but much more needed to be done. Even more crucial, it was not clear what the congregation would be in the future—how it would be the body of Christ in its place and time. As this chapter shows, there are no guarantees that a congregation in crisis will inevitably be able to reverse its fortunes. Especially during the interim period, the future seemed up in the air, with much anxiety about where the church would end up.

On the other hand, it would be irresponsible simply to dismiss the possibility of Adrift becoming a healthy congregation. Adrift may be able to find itself, call an appropriate senior pastor and return to the level of mission (although perhaps not in the same direction) as in its past. To understand the story of this congregation, we begin with the history before examining the present crisis—a crisis that I think was finally an issue of identity and mission.

Background

Adrift Lutheran Church was founded in 1923 in the heart of a large metropolitan city. Although it flourished during its early years, changes in the traffic patterns in the city isolated the church so that it was largely inaccessible, and membership declined. By 1956 the church decided to relocate, and when the pastor left for another call, the time was ripe for the move. The old church building was sold. About 30 members and $100,000 (that is $655,000 in 2001 dollars) accompanied the church as it sought to call a new pastor and find a new beginning.

The missions board of the national Lutheran church called a young man, Karl Opportune, fresh from seminary, to develop the congregation in a small town/suburban setting that was exploding in growth, located just northeast of the city. Karl conducted the first service at this location in the local fire hall on Reformation Sunday, October 28, 1956, with 155 people attending. Thus began a saga of 42 years of productive ministry by Karl in this congregation. Mission developers within my denomination often say that a mission start can expect to grow between five and 10 times the size of its initial Sunday worship. Adrift would eventually post an average worship attendance of 1500—10 times the size of its first service. But size does not tell the story of the impact and influence of this congregation.

Karl Opportune's approach to the Christian faith and ministry was different from that of most Lutheran pastors. At the beginning of his ministry Karl came under the influence of the New York-based pastor and writer Norman Vincent Peale and the "power of positive thinking." With the ensuing years he became a friend both of Dr. Peale and of Robert H. Schuller, the California minister who has emphasized "possibility theology." In this regard, Karl broke away from the more somber Germanic Lutheran theology of his pastor father and his theology professors, with its emphasis on sin and forgiveness.

By the mid-1970s, Dr. Opportune had developed his *Opportunity Seekers' Creed*: "Life is for living! If it gets comfortable I will not coast.

If it becomes empty or dark I will strike a new match of opportunity and with God's help move forward in its light." In 1976, Karl published his first book, *Make It Happen*, with a foreword commending the book by Schuller of the "Crystal Cathedral" in Garden Grove, California. His book begins with these words:

> There are no difficulties in life—
> only opportunities.
> There are no disappointments in life—
> only opportunities.
> There are no disasters in life—
> only opportunities.
> There are no problems in life—
> only opportunities. . . .
> But I am convinced
> that every difficulty
> every problem
> every disaster
> every disappointment
> is a diamond mine—
> if you are rightly related
> to Jesus Christ—
> if you are open and receptive
> to his power in your life
> to guide and direct you.

Karl followed that book with another in 1979, *Choose to Win*, which further elaborated his philosophy of positive thinking. In 1977, Pastor Opportune developed a *Make It Happen* television series, a vehicle for espousing an "opportunity attitude." His philosophy can be seen also in the plaque Karl had placed in the seventh elderly-housing complex he built: "With work, pain, and love this place was built for you! What this place will become depends on you. My prayer is you will share a smile, give a hand, be a friend and these halls will ring with happiness and friendship, but more, there will be a smile on the face of our Lord—[signed] Karl Opportune."

Members talked about him as a powerful, dynamic speaker and preacher. One said his vision was "all things are possible with God," while another expressed it as, "God is with you, God loves you, use your gifts . . .

make something of yourself." Still another saw Karl's central message as "climbing your mountains with opportunity seeking as your attitude. There are no problems in life, just opportunities." Finally, another member summarized Karl's impact: "It was a pulpit church led by a visionary leader who had the ability to realize his vision in lots of ways."

And people flocked to hear this message, especially in an affluent neighborhood where, by 2001, few homes were available for under $250,000. In fact, in an occupational profile of members done in a self-study by Adrift in 2000, the average household income of the members was calculated to be $131,000, and 38 percent of the members had a college education or more. One member said that Karl's message gave hearers "permission to be successful in the world." Another said that "people felt as though they were charged up and ready to go." Yet, another noted that Karl's message was attractive to people from all denominations. It made people feel good and left them motivated not only to climb another mountain, but also to feel capable of doing just "a little bit more," by extending a helping hand to those in need.

What didn't get talked about was sin. One member suggested that Karl's message appealed to some people who came from churches that attracted "sin-based, guilt-ridden" people, who "loved to come here because they felt so good after he spoke to them." Another member agreed: "I always liked coming here with Pastor Opportune. He realized what went on in real life. He wasn't above you and he didn't just preach the Bible. He dealt with what went on in real life." His favorite Bible story was the parable of the prodigal son, emphasizing the forgiveness and saving help of the father even when the son had not repented. He used this sermon so much that, to honor Karl, the congregation erected a large statue of the father and the prodigal son in front of the church.

But another member suggested that Karl was selective in his use of scriptural texts, emphasizing the healing ministries and the miracles of Jesus, with Karl seeing his message as akin to what Jesus preached and taught. But he would not talk about the cross, judgment, confession, or sin. "He never really preached the Bible," a member said. "He mentioned it, but then went on with real-life situations." Another suggested that Karl preached "Sunday-morning psychology." Members also said he did not preach very frequently from Paul or the Old Testament.

In a conversation with me, Karl said that we are called to follow Jesus' example: "Paul, after all, had never really known Jesus and was just working out of the theology of the Jewish church at that time." Instead Karl focused on Jesus' teachings and actions. "What did he do? He went around helping and healing and uplifting the people. He worked with the downcasts, the crooked politicians, and the outcasts of society, and gave them hope. Jesus never worked with just church people, except to condemn them for their empty religiosity." Karl compared worship to a spiritual filling station where people come to be filled with the word so that they can go out and expend that fuel in helping others.

It is important to note, however, that he did not just talk about helping others; he carried it out in his leadership of Adrift and in his relationships with others on the staff. One member concluded about this vision: "It was his vision, his church. He was a wonderful pastor. When he was here, he did a lot of outreach programs to the community. He was always around to help somebody. He would always work something out. If you didn't like something, talk to him."

Moreover, his outreach and service to the community found many avenues. In 1962 Karl saw a definite need for a nursery school where children could develop their social and basic-learning skills. It opened with an initial enrollment of 14 but expanded rapidly and served 250 children by 1981. Today, the preschool has 220 children and 24 full-time staff. It is one of the largest preschools in the area, offering two-and-a-half-hour sessions, with an extended day if the parents need it. While the school has a waiting list, it is not yet a day-care center.

In 1967, the church opened a community youth center called "The Spot After." On Tuesday nights, organized "rap" sessions covered relevant subjects. Daily it was a place to watch TV or just sit and talk to friends. On Friday nights, The Spot After hosted dances with live bands. It held family-film nights on Saturday and turnabout nights when teenagers entertained their parents. While The Spot After no longer exists, it was quite the gathering place for teenagers in the late '60s and early '70s.

In 1969, Karl Opportune, in partnership with a local housing contractor, built the first senior-citizen housing complex, and named it Adrift Towers. By the time of my interviews, Karl and his business associate had opened seven senior citizen housing projects in the neighborhood of Adrift Church. Some of these units have used federal Housing and Urban Development (HUD) money and house the poor and underprivileged, while one is upscale and intended for the affluent of the area. Most of these complexes have the name of the church as part of their title. For years, most members of the congregation thought that the complexes were a direct ministry of the church. Indeed, these housing complexes *were* part of the outreach ministry of the church, but only indirectly. These projects were legally formed into a 501(c)(3) (nonprofit) corporation called Adrift Outreach, with Karl as chief executive officer. Karl incorporated them separately from the congregation because of the great danger of failure and bankruptcy during the early years, and also because he felt the need to keep them separate so that the wider Lutheran church could not take the projects over, as part of its large social-ministry network. At the time of the interviews, Karl had plans made to develop two more housing complexes.

In the mid-1970s, member requests for counseling became more than Karl could handle, so he led the church to open a counseling clinic, called Growth Opportunity Center. He hired a clinical psychologist, who was a member of Adrift, to head this agency to provide counseling that was both high-quality and affordable for church members and area residents. From this humble beginning to the present, under the direction of the same clinical psychologist, the center rapidly expanded. It became self-supporting in two years and shortly thereafter became self-incorporated, a step that freed the church from liability and enabled the center to work with public schools. The center treated those with and without insurance; those without insurance were charged on a sliding scale, depending on their income. In 2001 the center, which rented buildings on Adrift's campus, employed more than 40 health professionals and averaged about 1,400 visits per month.

The members were proud of all this outreach into the community, enthusiastic about their church, and devoted to their dynamic senior minister. Consequently new members continued to flock to the church. In addition to these huge projects, the congregation ardently carried out many smaller ministries. During the 1970s Adrift sponsored three families of refugees from Vietnam. In fact, Karl awarded the first sponsored Vietnamese family the Opportunity Attitude Award in 1981 for courage in overcoming many hardships to become successful and valuable members of American society. Another outreach program begun in the 1970s, the Creative Arts Center, offered 30 adult enrichment courses, from writing and psychology to quilting and aerobics. "Friends," a singles ministry, started for members and community residents, drew 125 men and women to their weekly meetings. A Job Opportunity Center assisted people in finding employment. "Fifty-Plussers" consisted of 1300 "experienced" citizens over 50 who sponsored enrichments programs and travel adventures. The church also held an annual series of concerts and lectures featuring people from business, politics, religion, and theater. Karl hired staff to lead these outreach ministries. The patriotic Karl held a gala celebration and services every July 4. For decades, a local radio station broadcast Karl's Sunday morning sermons. Finally, in recent years, Karl led Adrift to help a synagogue that was having financial difficulties.

By 1960 the congregation had grown to 416 members and assumed full financial responsibility for itself, ending its status as a mission church. Of course, the growth in membership necessitated building and enlarging the church complex. By 1961, the congregation had assumed its permanent home and built a beautiful sanctuary. In 1993, Adrift completed its sixth expansion program initiated during Karl's pastorate.

Just as the physical plant needed to expand, so did the staff to serve the church and its missions. The first assistant pastor was called in 1964, less than eight years after Adrift had restarted itself in a fire hall. In 1975, Adrift broke new ground by calling as director of parish life a minister of another denomination (Presbyterian). By the mid-1990s the staff included senior pastor, teaching pastor (full-time), youth pastor (full-time), pastoral-care pastor (part-time), secretary to the senior pastor (full-time), three administrative assistants (full-time), director of public relations (full-time), director of Christian education (full-time), director of women's ministries (part-time), coordinator of volunteers (part-time), and a computer/technical assistant consultant (full-time). The unusual number of employees did not escape members' notice. "Adrift is different in that the staff ran the programs, not the volunteers," said a member. "In most other churches, the volunteers run the programs. Karl always had it that the staff ran the programs." Karl's method of building his staff was to find someone who had the capabilities but who also might be in a difficult situation due to divorce, death of spouse, or inability to find the right job. Then, Karl would offer them an appropriate position with the congregation.

In contrast to this successful ministry, Karl Opportune maintained a strained relationship with the larger Lutheran church body, especially with the synod (the regional judicatory) that was headquartered in the city. Karl was the son of a prominent German Lutheran pastor who at one time had served as pastor of the largest German Lutheran congregation in this city, a congregation noted for its strong and innovative social ministries. But just as he had broken from his father's theology, so he broke his close ties to the denomination of which he was a part. The congregation did not use the

Lutheran Book of Worship—or any other official Lutheran hymnal or liturgy. Instead, the church used a 1950s-era hymnal not affiliated with any denomination. The Sunday liturgy was one Karl designed especially for this church. Moreover, Karl did not attend annual synod conventions; nor did he send lay representatives. During Karl's tenure, Adrift paid very little benevolence money to the wider Lutheran church, preferring to use the money for local missions of its own choosing. Since members came from diverse religious backgrounds, I think Adrift was Lutheran largely in name only. Nevertheless, Karl always kept Lutheran in the name of the church, and never tried to separate the congregation from the Lutheran denomination (now the ELCA).

Several interviewees described Karl's leadership style as that of a benevolent dictator, while others said he was more like the CEO of a company, and one person even compared Karl to a mythical figure. "With Karl it was like when King Arthur built his court, his perfect world. The leaders sat at the round table, and they were in Utopia." Members said that Adrift was *the* church to attend, the rich church on the corner that did exciting ministry and had all those programs. One member, now in his mid-20s, remembers that during his high school years in the community, he felt as if everybody was "either a part of a Jewish synagogue [there is a significant Jewish population in the neighborhood] or you belonged to Adrift."

Interviewees also suggested that Karl's leadership style worked because he had a vision for the congregation: The church should be a healer and helper to those in need. He knew how to communicate that vision to the people of Adrift, and he could turn the vision into action with excellent, exciting results. "He was very good with people. He didn't belittle people, and he would affirm the work of people in their professions. He was able to work with people who were powerful in their field. He got them to buy into his vision. It worked because he was a great guy." A staff member offered a professional perspective: "He was very, very, very creative. He would do the impossible. He really supported women. He could find whomever he needed for a job and always found someone who needed help. You became indebted to him and worked your heart out."

One thing Karl did *not* do was to prepare the congregation for the day when he would no longer be their pastor, though he tried. He intended to prepare the church by handpicking his successor. But he failed to make a clean break with the congregation when that successor arrived. In the end, at Karl's retirement, the congregation fell into a long, sustained period of crises.

The Crises

Karl Opportune envisioned how the transition to his retirement would take place: He would bring in a younger pastor who could reach the young people to continue the proud ministry he had been doing for 42 years. But according to several interviewees, in the last years of Karl's ministry, attendance at Adrift began to erode slowly, as did the financial picture. To meet its obligations, Adrift drew money from the memorial funds until they were depleted, and then the congregation had to establish a line of credit with a bank. Meanwhile, members said, Karl realized he was not reaching the young families with children or young people as he had throughout his earlier ministry. Karl was over 65. Thus, he wanted to bring in a younger pastor who understood and agreed with his vision for the church and would carry it on.

Interviewees concurred that Karl "handpicked" his successor, the Rev. Harold Tidings, who had been a well-liked, dynamic youth and singles-ministry pastor at Adrift from 1981 to 1984 immediately upon graduation from seminary. Harold himself called Karl "my pastor and my mentor." The two remained close friends after Harold left Adrift to serve another congregation in the area. When Harold worked on a doctor of ministry degree, he asked Karl to be the outside resource person on the doctoral committee. In fact, it was Karl who submitted Harold's name to a large congregation in the Midwest because he thought Harold possessed the leadership qualities that the church needed. Thus, when Karl considered retirement, he telephoned Pastor Harold Tidings and asked him to think about coming back. Conversations between the two continued for a year until official steps were taken to call Harold to Adrift as senior pastor. Though Harold had invited Karl to go to the Midwest to see his ministry there, the associate pastor—not Karl—made the trip. One interviewee suggested that if Karl had gone, he might have realized how different Harold's ministry was from his own and recognized that the two were incompatible. But confident in his close relationship with Harold, Karl had him called to Adrift.

When Harold arrived in May 1998, Adrift's leadership and ministry quickly became conflictual. First of all, Harold's theological bent had changed since his years as a youth pastor. "Harold had changed since I knew him from being here the first time," said one member. "Harold brought a more traditional, much more Christ-oriented, much more evangelical approach." Several members observed that in his first sermon, Harold mentioned Jesus 13 times—someone was alleged to have counted! One member said that some congregants were upset that Harold carried a Bible. Another said he came from "the Bible belt and biblical theology." Other people complained about his style from the pulpit—that he was loud and animated, with a few even suggesting that they "expected to see him tap dancing up there."

Second, conflict arose over who was in charge. Several of the members I interviewed said that Karl thought he and Harold would work as a team; Karl would "still call the shots, preach once a month, and find a way to maintain Adrift the way he wanted." Harold had developed into a creative leader himself, and he made it clear that he was going to be his own leader. Moreover, disagreement flared over the senior pastor's office. Harold arrived in May, but Karl did not vacate the corner office until October. Also, Karl chaired church council meetings until October. Harold had expected that Karl would be away for much of the summer, during which time Harold would become established. In a conversation with me, Karl stated that he had made it clear that he would not leave his office until October. Karl also told me that the model he wanted to emulate was Dr. Norman Vincent Peale and the way Peale continued to be an active leader in his congregation after his retirement. Even when Karl vacated his office in October, he was not far away. Adrift Outreach, the nonprofit organization caring for the housing complexes, of which Karl was CEO, rented space in a house belonging to the church literally up the hill, above the church. So, according to one interviewer, even in retirement, "Karl could look down on the church from his office."

Conflict erupted in the church. Some people welcomed Harold's change in leadership and preaching. Others wanted to keep Karl's styles of preaching and leading the church. The church council became divided because several members were loyal to Karl. Harold wanted the council to assume its rightful independence and power, but relations soured. "They started to micromanage and became combative with Harold," one member said. "He gave them the power; they went a step further to abuse that." Another member said, "Some people wanted Karl still to be involved and didn't understand that you can't run a marriage with the father-in-law living in the house."

Competing loyalties to each pastor split Adrift. "I really got the impression that you had to choose between Karl and Harold," said one member. Another called the conflict a matter of trust. Many members "trusted Karl Opportune, but when he resigned, they didn't trust the pastor who came. They don't trust the church council now. Some follow Karl, some follow Harold; and some follow the intentional interim minister." Interviewees suspect that Karl felt he might have made a wrong choice, and similar sentiments began to surface among his followers.

Seventeen months after Harold Tidings came, he resigned. In a letter to the congregation, dated October 25, 1999, Harold stated:

> I came to Adrift with the hope that we could chart a new course of ministry for this place. I believe I brought from my pastoral experiences a firm grasp of what it takes to provide transition for a church. One of the central dynamics of transition is support from those with whom you work. Although there have been people who have embraced with excitement the ministry opportunities God has brought to this church, there also has been a very intense effort to derail the ministry.

Harold complimented the professional staff for its very positive spirit. Then he continued,

> Recently, the congregation and a portion of the Church Council have rallied positive support for the ministry God has entrusted to this place. There is, though, a portion of our Church Council that has not shown support. It is also important to recognize that the most disruptive aspect that has gotten in the way of future growth is the non-support shown by Pastor Karl Opportune. . . . I believe that by resigning at this time, I am allowing the issues of nonsupportive leadership and the interference by past pastoral leadership to be dealt with and analyzed.

Harold suggested that Adrift would have trouble finding future pastoral leadership until the issue of past pastoral presence was dealt with.

The backlash from this letter came immediately. Members close to Karl perceived that he had been driven from the church. A number of them stopped coming to church themselves and withheld their offerings. Many of these were among the biggest contributors to the church. On the other side were members who had appreciated and benefited from the ministry of Harold Tidings and who perceived that Karl and his supporters had undermined his ministry from the beginning and had driven him to resign. They were angry toward Karl and those loyal to him. A third group wanted simply to worship God and have no part in the conflict. Some transferred to other churches while others decided just to stay away until the crisis had passed or until they saw who the next pastor would be. One interviewee estimated that worship attendance had slipped from about 1300 worshipers or more a week in 1993 to 550 people a week in early 2001. Another felt that weekly attendance was half what it had been four years previously.

The bishop's office took three actions immediately after Harold's resignation. First, the bishop and Pastor Karl Opportune jointly sent a letter to all members of Adrift. "We write to you because we share a common concern for the welfare of Adrift. . . . We both believed Pastor Harold Tidings would effectively lead Adrift into the next century. He has decided that this is not the appropriate course for his life and ministry. Neither of us imagined that the congregation would face such a time of crisis." Acknowledging that they stood in different places, both men were heartsick over the spirit of discord threatening the future, the letter said. "People who once were friends suddenly are not speaking to each other. We ask you to find a way to overcome this and bring healing to Adrift."

Next, the bishop and Pastor Opportune pledged to help. The bishop (and his staff) promised to work faithfully to find an appropriate interim minister and to work with Adrift until the church called a new senior pastor. Karl promised to support the interim process as it moved forward under the leadership of the church council and synod. Karl reminded them that "as a retired pastor, I do not officiate in ministerial functions." In fact, Karl and his wife did not worship at Adrift after the writing of this letter.

The third action by the bishop and his staff was to insist that Adrift enter a period with an intentional interim minister rather than try to call a senior pastor. And the bishop went as far as the Upper Midwest to find an intentional interim with the ability and training to be most helpful in this difficult situation. Meanwhile, at Adrift seven of the 12 church council members who had been supporters of Karl Opportune resigned. Some members called the remaining council members "the fabulous five." They bore the burden of providing leadership for the church, especially in the three-month period before the intentional interim minister could arrive.

Intentional Interim Minister

Mark Empower is a lifelong midwesterner. Ordained in 1976, he served two regular calls between 1976 and 1989. The last seven years of that period were in a conflicted situation, requiring redevelopment work, and so he began to use his continuing education time for training in the dynamics of interim ministry, especially in conflict resolution, mediation in multiple-staff situations, and grief and loss in corporate settings. Significantly in his development, he spent a year (1989–1990) as a full-time residency student in clinical pastoral education. This year of CPE training was particularly important because he was to use many of the skills of a CPE supervisor in his work at Adrift. In 1991, he began his intentional interim work, and in 1998 he began a doctor of ministry program with a focus on "leadership in congregations in transition." Adrift was his fourth intentional interim call. Mark was not only a member of the Interim Ministry Network but also a member of the National Association of Lutheran Interim Pastors.

The bishop in the East with oversight of Adrift Lutheran had a high regard for the work of intentional interims, learned of Mark's name and qualifications, and asked Mark to interview with him and his staff. After the interviews, the bishop recommended Mark as the intentional interim for Adrift. Mark began on February 1, 2000, as full-time interim senior pastor. Because he continued to live in the Upper Midwest, he and church leaders worked out a schedule for him to spend three weeks at Adrift and one week off. The agreement was for 12 months. The letter of agreement from the synod listed seven areas in which Mark would lead the congregation. In conversations between Mark and the church council, an additional nine areas were singled out.

Seven new council members had been elected to join the "fabulous five." In the first months, Mark focused with the leadership on the topic "How we can come together as leaders and model the Body of Christ?" The two-thirds new council needed to learn to know and trust one another and jell as a team. Even though the council met weekly in the early days of the interim ministry, Mark scheduled a retreat in two parts: Near the end of April 2000, the council spent a day and a half working with an outside consultant to become a team and to begin to frame a vision. In mid-May, the consultant led the council in a six-hour Sunday afternoon retreat. By the end of these retreats trust had developed among the council members. In June, they drafted a mission statement. Mark was on vacation during that month, and the drafting was led by the associate pastor, the Rev. Bob Friend. Almost everyone I interviewed said that the mission statement had stayed on the wall but had not reached the hearts of the parishioners. Members ignored the mission statement—another signal that the congregation did not have a common identity or a shared vision.

When Mark returned in July, he began to work individually with council members as they exercised their leadership positions. He voiced concern about the congregation's ability to move forward, given the current staffing arrangements, but the council rejected his ideas for possible pastoral staff changes. A minority of the council began to question whether Mark was the person to lead them through the interim. Mark, of course, also worked with the staff and often functioned as a messenger between the staff and the council. Turmoil and conflict continued in the congregation between those who wanted Karl invited back in some capacity; some who wanted a pastor like Harold, and some who wanted the council to hurry up and bring in a permanent senior pastor. In December 2000, Adrift's leadership finished its congregational self-study. It is standard procedure among Lutherans for the bishop to wait for the self-study to be completed before authorizing a congregation to form a call committee to search for a new pastor. Adrift's self-study done, the bishop gave his permission. Meanwhile, time was running short on Mark's one-year contract with the congregation. The bishop urged that Mark be continued on a month-to-month basis. Yet, a new conflict arose over the effectiveness of the intentional interim senior pastor. The congregation was split over Mark's ministry, and that was reflected in the close council vote to renew his contract.

During 2000, Adrift's financial woes continued because income remained depressed, and it became obvious that the congregation would be short $155,000 by year's end. At a congregation meeting on November 19, members gave the council permission to balance the proposed 2001 budget by making cuts.

In early January 2001, the council reached a balanced budget by cutting one or two staff positions and by halving the hours of several others. Anger exploded again. The staff members were upset because they felt the council had not consulted with them about where the cuts would be made. Some would have been willing to reduce their time voluntarily so that others could retain their hours. Adrift's members did not realize that giving permission to balance the budget would mean staff reductions. Most pointedly, the council had halved the hours of a beloved staff person who had headed her area of ministry for 30 years; she was widely perceived as one of the saviors of the congregation during the recent difficult times. In turn, she chose to resign rather than accept the reduction (thinking she could not do her job adequately in half the time). Many people said they would leave the church if she didn't continue in her position.

In a letter of January 11, 2001, a couple in the congregation proposed a solution they dubbed "Operation 2001 Deficit Reduction." Explaining that they thought the intent of the November 19 meeting was for the church council to find ways to increase revenues, not to cut staff hours to reduce expenses, the couple offered to match one dollar for every two dollars raised, up to giving $100,000. They attached 10 stipulations to the offer. For example, the council must approve this endeavor at its January 15 meeting, or the offer would be withdrawn. The period for collecting the money would be the three months after January 15. All terminations and reductions would be immediately cancelled, and all affected personnel restored to previous status/benefits. The staff members would be guaranteed their positions through 2002, as long as job performance maintained previous standards. After considerable discussion on January 15, the council accepted this proposal. Within the three-month period, $222,000 was raised and, when the couple added their $100,000, the total came to $322,000. All staff positions were returned to their previous level.

By spring 2001, the call committee was working with names of potential candidates for senior pastor; in early July it made an offer to a candidate to meet with the council and congregation. At that point, however, the candidate withdrew, citing the financial instability of the congregation.

In July, yet another eruption rocked the congregation. Mark and the support staff had planned special celebrations during the fall to commemorate the 45th birthday of the congregation. Part of the plan called for six former pastors or sons of the congregation to return on Sundays during the fall, with Mark preaching on the culminating Sunday. However, a delegation from the congregation approached the council, saying that if Dr. Opportune returned to the pulpit, they would leave the church and withdraw their offerings. The council decided not to commemorate the anniversary in this way, and the plans were scuttled. Again, when this eruption occurred, a few more people stopped coming to church, with some people telling Mark, "I can't worship here any more."

Because of the continued conflict, on August 19, Mark Empower preached a sermon titled "Blazing New Trails." In it, he pointed to Jesus' command to "love our enemies: "But you know what happens to people who strive to love their enemies? Yes, we crucify them! It is interesting to remember that Jesus was crucified, not because he was a lawgiver. He was crucified because he was a love giver. Jesus was blazing a new trail in which to live. That trail is ours to follow each day of our lives." After referring to the movie *Love Story*—the book on which it was based is the source of the catchy phrase "Love means never having to say you're sorry"—Mark pointed out that this statement is absolutely contrary to Christian understanding and belief. For Christians, love means saying, "I'm sorry."

> In every congregation that I have served, I believe that these words apply: "I'm sorry. . . ." There can be divisions. The divisions can escalate and "camps" are developed. "Sides" are taken. They say, "we are for those" or " we are against that." Many words can be spoken in haste. Proposals can be made and counter proposals offered. . . .
>
> I believe that here at Adrift it is time to say, "I'm sorry" to one another. I believe that we need to speak those words out loud, or at least symbolically. We need to hear those words in this sanctuary, in the Garden Room, in the hallways. We need to exercise sacrificial love in the chapel, in the parking lot and in our homes in order for a crisis to be avoided. We need to say, "I'm sorry" and swallow our pride. It is time.
>
> I throw down the challenge of reconciliation. It is the only way out! And if the differences are not resolved, and the rumors and innuendos continue and the proposals keep coming up, no one wins and all lose. More importantly, if reconciliation is not striven for and lived toward and not resolved, there will be a crucifixion of a community. Let's choose another trail. Let's blaze it after the One who blazed it for us.

According to Mark, the sermon helped the spirit of cooperation within the congregation. However, with the bishop's blessing, Mark knew that the time for him to leave had come. "I have become too much a part of the system to bring about any more lasting turnaround." On September 30, 2001, Mark submitted his resignation, and his last Sunday at Adrift was October 14. He had been the intentional interim for 19 months.

Dynamics of the Intentional Interim Period

The issue of congregational identity and lack of shared vision were key issues within Adrift in the fall of 2001. Asked what issues were facing this congregation, one member put it succinctly: "Trust, vision, leadership, and communication—those jump out. They are all interrelated." I agree, for these are the elements that make up an identity, mutually agreed upon. Let us now turn to the dynamics that made trust, vision, leadership, and communication such issues. Many factors contributed.

First, when Karl announced his retirement, most members experienced a great sense of loss that he would no longer be part of the congregation. However, there was never a clean closure, never a time to celebrate the last 42 years and the retirement of the only pastor most of this congregation had ever known. Instead, Karl became a big part of the conflict, and people felt they needed to choose sides for or against Karl. A lot of the continued eruption and anger occurred because the congregation never experienced closure with the former pastor.

Some members thought there would be no closure any time soon. "It is going to take years," one member said, to move beyond Karl's presence, maybe even "until Karl is dead." Another disagreed: "Karl is less of an issue for many. I think we are ready to move ahead." The intentional interim tended to agree with the latter statement. It has been almost three years since Karl has set foot in the church. Moreover, while hurt, Karl did want the church to move forward. In fact, although Mark did not approach Karl during the first seven months of his interim ministry, Mark did set up an appointment, and he and Karl had a frank and fruitful conversation. With communication restored, Karl became supportive of Mark's ministry and encouraged those who were close to him to work with Mark, even though Mark's theological position was far different from Karl's.

One group of Adrift members of German background (Karl's father emigrated from Germany to be a pastor in America.) met monthly away from the church after Karl's retirement, and Karl met with them. For the last year of his ministry, Mark attended the meetings of this group, because he was, in his terms, called to bring "unity reconciliation." Of course, the very fact that he would attend these meetings angered the anti-Karl segment.

The next senior pastor will need to be cognizant of those who have been loyal to Karl and encourage them to become active again in the life of the congregation. The new pastor would be well advised to meet with Karl, as Mark did, and reach an understanding with him. Karl is not the detriment to ministry that he was when Harold Tidings came. The interim minister has provided a buffer from the previous pastor so that now the ministry can more readily move forward, if the congregants can agree on a direction.

A second issue playing out was Adrift's identity as a Lutheran church. One interviewee said, "People feel we are Lutheran." However, Karl always kept the wider Lutheran church at a distance, and did not participate in the yearly synod meetings nor send lay representatives to these meetings. Adrift has been represented by both clergy and laity only since Karl's retirement. Furthermore, Karl's theology was not characteristically Lutheran. I say this because at the very heart of Lutheran theology stands the gospel—the good news of what God is doing for us in Jesus Christ, while we are yet sinners. Because of our ongoing sin, the cross and resurrection of Jesus provide forgiveness on our behalf. Our calling is to "take up the cross and follow Jesus." Karl's opportunity theology focuses, not so much on sin and forgiveness, but rather on serving our neighbor in need, being Christ-like to our neighbor. Moreover, Adrift did not use the *Lutheran Book of Worship*, nor did the congregation support the Lutheran church well through benevolence gifts. However, Harold Tidings worked closely with the synod during his 19 months as pastor, and the bishop and his office were closely involved both in selecting and in supporting Mark during his interim ministry. The congregation still needs to sort out the level of its commitment to the Lutheran church, including the use of Lutheran worship books and Christian education material.

A third dynamic was the associate pastor, Bob Friend, who had been at Adrift for almost 11 years and was well liked and respected by the members and leaders of the congregation. Bob described himself as an evangelical who came from Wheaton College, and came out of a Presbyterian church to become a pastor at Adrift. Bob and Mark had not always agreed about the direction of ministry at Adrift. Bob himself said, "I have been here a long time; I am a new pastor's worse nightmare. I don't want to be, and I struggle with that. We have tried to hash things out and address issues." Bob felt he had been cut off from a lot of decision making during the interim. For example, he told me that he had not been consulted about the staff cuts. Moreover, many congregational members and a portion of the leadership felt that Bob would have been the best choice as the interim minister, and that Adrift did not need to go to the expense of hiring an outside intentional interim. Because Bob was not Lutheran, the bishop had insisted that Adrift have a Lutheran intentional interim who was especially trained to minister in conflicted situations. In my opinion, the relationship the new senior pastor develops with Bob will be critical for the start of his or her ministry at Adrift because Bob has so much support in the congregation.

A fourth factor was Mark's style and the degree to which he did or did not meet the expectations of the congregation. There is no question that his ministry was controversial. "It has been a rocky year," a council member responded when asked to evaluate the interim minister. "Some think he is good, some don't. We have had a deliberate process, and [he has] guided us and that is good. Mark has helped us to be able to get ready to face change." Two interviewees said specifically that half the people like Mark and half complain about him. One person said,

> I don't accept that we needed an interim. We could have had guest speakers, or Pastor Friend could have done a lot. I really don't see what Mark has done except to try to have a balanced budget. I really can't see any difference. The church has not really moved in another direction since he has been here. . . . I think we are ready to call a senior pastor. That is what everybody wants. We have been going through what the synod requests, but there is nothing better in the past year with Mark.

Some interviewees suggested that Mark had not been fully accepted by the council, the staff, or the people. One council member admitted that Mark tried to place decision making in the hands of the council, but when Mark would make suggestions or recommendations, the council would question, "Does he have a good grasp with the history? He hasn't been here as long as we have and doesn't know the personalities. Then you question what he suggests, and you get into the trust issue. It is a real Catch-22."

Another leader described the way members were visiting other churches, changing membership, or waiting to see who the new pastor would be. "The greatest need is to get a senior pastor and get a new direction, because the congregation won't listen to the direction set by the council or interim pastor. They think we are leaderless." Two interviewees were even more blunt: "The congregation needs a scapegoat—that is Mark." Another said that some people don't understand the function of interim ministry and that "those people will blame the interim for 90 percent of the problems anyway." These comments are good examples of reactionary anger from a segment of the congregation when there are no immediate solutions to the strife. Some people long for the new messianic leader who will arrive as senior pastor and tell the congregants how the church will be.

Several people remarked about Mark's style. "He has been a wildly different pastor compared to our past senior pastors. Both Karl and Harold were much more outgoing, more energetic, more 'take-control.' Mark has been very passive as far as leadership is concerned. Harold and Karl were much more dynamic in the pulpit, very different from Mark." But later in the interview the same person conceded, "My perception is that Mark's quiet demeanor and smoothness with people is maybe, in fact, exactly what should be happening here." Another council member said,

> I respect Mark. We have batted heads like oil and water. We are different managers. I am aggressive and Mark is very passive, . . . and he sits back to let situations solve themselves. We are in so much turmoil and debates. I try to mediate them and I sometimes make them worse. Mark sits back and lets things happen. We need a strong, powerful leader. . . . We have come a long way and made progress, but not like we should. I respect Mark for all that he has done. Being an interim pastor is a thankless job.

Another person also thought the church needed a more decisive, strong leader: "Mark has assumed the consulting role, and the church is expecting a leader role. Council is expected to step up into the leader role."

On the other hand, many interviewees fully supported Mark and his style. At the beginning of this chapter I quoted the member who said Mark was a deliberative leader who was forcing the council and congregation to take control of the church. One person said simply that it was "nice to have a neutral person to oversee everything." Another said Mark helped the members look to one another for leadership. "It is time for each of us to contribute to the church and not sit on the coattails of other people," he said. "There used to be priorities not in order. He is guiding us with the best changeovers as he sees fit." Another saw clearly the advantage of having an interim minister: "It was necessary to have the intentional interim. If we had gone that route from the beginning, we would not have sacrificed Harold. If we were to call Harold now, instead of in the beginning, he would be wonderful for us." This same member added:

Mark has helped us slow things down and helps us do tasks by educating us with the way it should be done. His basics are to slow down, redefine our mission, and develop a clearer idea of what the church is looking for. . . . He has helped the people grieve the loss of what had been and not act out . . . those feelings, but get through them. He has helped the congregation come together with a more common mission. Many feel we are going too slowly. Some of us realize that the deliberate slowness is essential.

In several interviews with Mark, I came to realize just how intentional was this approach at Adrift. Some of the leaders criticized him for what they perceived as his passivity, but any of us who have had a unit of clinical pastoral education can picture Mark as CPE supervisor—deliberately quiet and thereby forcing the group to take responsibility for itself and its future. Mark's "passivity" was intentional.

Mark told me that as an outside trained person, he had been able to determine the basic identity of the congregation very quickly, but that it didn't do him any good to tell it to them or to tell them how the identity needed to be changed. The council and the church needed to wrestle with these issues and come to their own conclusions. He explains:

Adrift has a long history of being a clergy-focused, staff-programmed congregation. They see themselves as . . . unique, on the cutting edge of the postmodern world. Through the years they believed they were light years ahead of other churches. Their theological base is extremely shallow, but they don't understand themselves in ecclesiastical or theological terms. Leaders of the congregation and many members view it as a business or a social community that should be run as a business.

Later in the interview Mark continued, "Identity for Adrift is primarily in doing rather than talking about what it is *to be* the body of Christ. Let's *do* the body of Christ; let's *do* ministry, rather than let's *be* the body of Christ." Mark saw part of his task to rediscover "what it is *to be*, so that what we *do* is consistent with who we are." Mark earmarked the identity issue as a major effort of his ministry. His aim always was to help the leadership struggle so it could say, "This is who we are and this is why we do what we do."

Many people wanted to short-cut this process, hoping instead to call a new, powerful, relevant leader to give them the vision. Mark likened such an attitude to saying, "Give us what we want; not necessarily what we need." Also, Mark recalled that some people would say, "We're not unified because you haven't unified us. We don't know our identity because you haven't told us that." Mark felt that there was little he could do except talk about the process and guide people through it.

Mark had a vision for the congregation, but he felt it would be counterproductive to try to impose it on the congregation. He stood ready to guide them through the process to see whether his concept of their identity would be one they accepted. He wanted Adrift to turn from a clergy-centered church to a congregation where the members step up to leadership positions and claim their rightful authority. Mark felt Adrift needed to change from a staff-programmed congregation to a church that equipped members for ministry themselves.

Future

I chose Adrift to illustrate that there are no guarantees of success simply because a congregation has an intentional interim minister. In the case of Adrift, I simply am not sure what will happen. Will this congregation become unified and healthy again? Will this congregation be able to call a senior pastor who fits its ministry needs? How can they honor the 42 years of ministry under Karl while turning in a different missional direction appropriate for the new century? How will the congregation live out its identity not only as the body of Christ but also as a Lutheran congregation?

As Mark Empower was leaving Adrift for a new intentional interim call in an affluent southern California suburb, he noted that he left with sadness for the 70 to 80 percent of the congregants who wanted the divisions to be over, for love to prevail, and for the people to be turned in unity to the future. He felt there was still a small minority of people with their own agendas for the congregation, and that whoever came as senior pastor would have to deal with that minority. On the positive side, the bishop was determined to work with Adrift until healthy missional ministry was restored there. As people of the resurrection, Christians are not optimistic but hopeful. Optimism is an emotion that changes like the weather from day to day. But Christians are always hopeful, because our God brings health from sickness and life where others perceive death.

Chapter 4

Established United Methodist Church

Heartland City, Midwest

In their first meeting with the congregation of Established United Methodist Church, one of the two intentional interim ministers told the congregants: "We have some good news/bad news for you this morning. If you like us, we will be here for only three years; if you don't like us, we will be here for only three years." Quoting this statement from memory, many interviewees said it had made a lasting impression on them. The announcement immediately set parameters around the ministry of the Revs. Judy Moderator and Marge Verve and accomplished exactly what the interims intended: Those who didn't like their style of ministry would be content to wait them out. Those who appreciated their ministry—by far the majority—knew that they were only paving the way for the next pastor.

One remarkable aspect of Established's situation was that a conference of the United Methodist Church chose to use intentional interim ministers in the first place. In most of the country, Methodists do not use these specially trained ministers for two reasons:

1. Interim appointments of odd lengths do not fit neatly with the Methodist polity of year-to-year, July-to-June, appointments; and

2. With the appointment system and the relatively shorter pastoral stays by Methodist ministers, a pastor can be a de facto interim by serving a church for only three years. In fact, the two senior pastors at Established who preceded the intentional interim team had each served for only a three-year period. The easiest "spot" for intentional interims to fit into Methodist polity is the emergency midyear appointment necessitated by a pastor's death, illness, or removal from office. But in this midwestern state, the judicatory has recognized the value of

specially trained ministers who make it their vocation to do only
intentional interim work.

As with Adrift Lutheran Church, the intentional interims were in place
when I studied the congregation, and like Adrift, this is a case with a
somewhat uncertain future. But there is at least one key difference between
the two churches. I chose "Established" as the name for this congregation
to convey both that it is deeply rooted in its community as one of the largest
churches there and because the members are overwhelmingly rooted in
their Methodism. Asked what kept them at Established, numerous
interviewees began by saying they were lifelong Methodists, or that they
liked the Methodist "system" and couldn't think about going to another
church. By "system," most meant the method and the frequency with which
clergy are deployed, how Methodist bishops and district superintendents
interact with congregations (it is an episcopal—hierarchical—system with
a human face), and a theology that focuses on serving one's neighbors.
This means that in part—and only in part—the identity issue is solved, and
Established does not have to discover how it will or will not be United
Methodist in the way Adrift has to decide how it will be a Lutheran
congregation.

On the other hand, no two United Methodist congregations have the
same identity. And since every church has to establish its unique identity,
Established had not completed that process when I was interviewing there.
The congregation also did not yet share a common vision for the future, but
instead had a kind of "wish list." Several members said they would like to
see a young male pastor with a wife and small children appointed, one who
could lead Established to grow by bringing in younger members and families
with children. This growth would have to contradict neighborhood
demographics, which were going in the opposite direction.

The Crisis

The conflict at Established reached its ignominious height in 1999 when a
petition was circulated asking for the removal of the two pastors—the
Revs. Peter Bowl and Sandra Dodge—and stating as reasons leadership
decisions without authorization, attempts to manage church funds not in
their power to manage, and ineptitude as pastoral leaders. Eventually 120

members signed this petition, and in the process, the petition was displayed at a business in town. The whole midwestern community learned about the problems at Established. Then, a few members took the petition to the district superintendent and bishop. When the time of year to appoint clergy to congregations came, the bishop and cabinet did not keep these pastors at Established. One member said that the bishop chose not to reappoint the senior pastor, Peter Bowl, out of fear for Peter's health, given the stress he was under, and Sandra Dodge, the assistant, as well.

Almost everyone interviewed suggested that I had to go back to the pastorate of the Rev. Landis Affable (1985–1993) to understand this crisis. Pastor Affable was a beloved pastor with what one interviewee called "a special talent to attract people, in the community as well as the church." He was "an outgoing, very personable man." He and his gregarious wife loved to entertain and had open houses for members. One person said Landis "treated everyone as a good friend of his. He was able to go with what the people wanted, with a smile on his face." Another said that he was "a take-charge guy and really got things done." Yet another suggested, "Day or night, anytime you needed him, he was there." Landis had an assistant pastor, a visitation pastor, and a dynamic youth minister to complement his leadership.

Several interviewees characterized Landis's social beliefs as out of sync with most of the members. "He was a liberal leader, and we had a fairly conservative congregation," one member said, "but he was able to say things in such a way that he ruffled some feathers, but they still respected him." Another agreed: "He was somebody that everybody liked. He didn't hesitate to say what he thought, and we all liked that." Yet another found his sermons challenging for their social positions, but that was OK. "He really gave you something to think about."

The one thing he did not do was delegate responsibilities, a penchant that did not equip the laity for leadership positions. "Some felt, if he does everything, what are we here for?" one member said. Two interviewees summed up the prevailing view of Pastor Affable: "People compare every pastor since to Landis Affable." And: "I always said the next minister to come along after Pastor Affable would have one foot in the grave, because the new minister could never match him."

The bishop appointed David Cultured (1993–1996) as the next senior pastor of Established. Pastor Cultured got in trouble with the congregation early on when he dismissed the visitation pastor who many years earlier had been the pastor of one of the two predecessor churches to Established. Actually, the groundwork for that pastor to leave had been laid under Pastor Affable, but some people chose to blame Pastor Cultured for this decision. Several people mentioned that Pastor Cultured was near retirement age and did not have the energy of a younger person. Also, his wife was not well. "She was very pleasant but physically unable to be active," commented one member—let alone entertain the way the Affables had. Several people found Affable's education and manner off-putting, suggesting he sometimes seemed "to talk down to people rather than to them." Others, however, found his manner authoritative. "He came across as a man who really commanded attention," said one. Everyone acknowledged that Pastor Cultured loved to tell stories both in sermons and in conversation. Some said he was the best preacher the congregation had had, while others thought his stories went on and on.

Members described Pastor Cultured as not being a warm, outgoing person. When immersed in a project, he disliked interruptions. "There were complaints he spent too much time on the computer." Several mentioned that he did not like to visit in homes, and some complained that he did not do enough hospital visitations. Others commented on his leadership style. "He didn't want to be involved with committees and didn't think they needed to function more than a couple of times a year." So the committees almost disappeared. "He ruffled a lot of feathers," one member said simply. Another summed it up: "There was only one way and that was David's way."

Two of his leadership decisions significantly irritated the congregation. First, although well educated, Pastor Cultured was not steeped in United Methodism. According to the interviewees, he urged the congregation not to pay apportionments to the wider church, but instead use the money for local projects. Apparently, the church did not even pay the apportionment for clergy support ministries, an indelible obligation of every United Methodist congregation. In fall 2001, when I made my research visit, the congregation had just taken most of the undesignated funds from its endowment ($70,000) to pay past-due apportionments for clergy support.

Second, Pastor Cultured wanted to energize the ministry to children and teenagers but forced—in the opinion of several interviewees—upon the congregation an outside candidate with questionable rapport with children. Apparently Pastor Cultured went outside United Methodism to find someone from an ecumenical, tent-maker group. "Certain people in the congregation applied for this position, but their names were never brought up before the leadership," said one member. "While a few really appreciated this young woman's ministry to teenagers, most felt that she did not relate to children from kindergarten the way a person in the position was asked to do. After two years, she was let go with hard feelings on both sides."

On the other hand, Pastor Cultured loved music and was very supportive of the choirs. In a church noted for its good music and especially its choir, he found a source of support in this area. Finally, toward the end of his ministry at Established, he hired as a lay visitation minister Sandra Dodge, a woman in her 30s who shortly obtained her license as a local pastor. In the United Methodist Church, certain leaders without college or seminary training can be appointed to a local congregation as pastor after fulfilling some coursework and other requirements of the judicatory. After three years as their pastoral leader, Pastor Cultured was not reappointed and subsequently retired.

After having a pastor near retirement age, members of Established had asked for and apparently expected a younger senior pastor. They were greatly disappointed. "I met Peter and thought he was the father of our new minister," said one member, describing his first encounter with Peter Bowl. "Peter was a major frustration for me," said another. "Our pastor-parish relations committee wanted a young energetic minister. Peter was looking at getting out of full-time ministry." Thus, Peter Bowl (1996-1999) had a major strike against him when he assumed the pastorate. Moreover, both his mother and his mother-in-law were ill and were cared for by Peter and his wife in the parsonage. Some interviewees said that Pastor Bowl "wasn't very easy to get to know." Other interviewees suggested that people skills were not his strength, and that he didn't relate well with youth. Two interviewees mentioned that he had trouble remembering names of parishioners. Apparently, a bit of an elitist attitude developed among some congregants who felt he lacked the education to lead the church. "This congregation has a lot of highly educated people," said one interviewee. "Some people made him feel he wasn't quite good enough." Another interviewee, however, pointed out that he was a kind man with compassion.

In the end, the three big issues fueling the crisis were finances, "contemporary" worship, and the qualifications of Sandra Dodge. According to one interviewee, Established had one of the largest endowments of any United Methodist congregation in the state, over $1 million. However, almost all of the funds were designated as to how they could be used. Several members echoed the frustration expressed by this interviewee: "We have a million dollars of endowments, but we can't pay our monthly bills." Pastor Bowl wanted to tap into this money for the programmatic needs of the church. He was especially upset that a specific endowment of $65,000 given in 1993, the Hughes Fund, with an annual income of $3,000, was to be used only for the music program of the church. Moreover, according to the terms of the bequest, the music committee, not the church council, was empowered to make all decisions about how this money was to be spent. Now it was contrary to United Methodist polity for a committee and not the congregation via a congregational meeting to have ultimate control over these funds, but a previous pastor and district superintendent had allowed the Hughes Fund to be set up legally under the sole control of the music committee.

Peter Bowl set up a separate committee, the contemporary worship committee, to look into establishing a contemporary service. He hoped the music committee would see the light, and free these funds for contemporary worship. In the process of trying to put this fund under the jurisdiction of the whole church via a congregational meeting, Peter attempted to do what could not be done legally. He even went to the Judicial Council of the United Methodist Church, the ultimate interpreter of church law, which further alienated the powerful music committee and many others involved in the musical programs of the church.

"Contemporary" was the word members used to describe this service. I have discovered that "contemporary" means different things in different churches. As one member described "contemporary" worship at Established to me, there is a synthesizer (electronic keyboard), but no guitar or drums. "We sing contemporary music," the member said. "The minister wears jeans and gives the sermon from a stool and not up in the pulpit." Another said the pastors put a dozen beanbag chairs around the chancel for this service. Meanwhile Peter and the music committee got tangled up in an issue of whether Peter was authorized to bring a synthesizer into the church, something he had done on a trial basis. Whatever the reality, many members perceived that he acted without authority. Many of the highly trained musicians regarded the synthesizer as a "thing" to be tolerated, not an instrument for good church music. After the synthesizer had been in the church for several months, the music committee decided that if a keyboard was to be bought for "contemporary" worship, it should be a good one, not the one Pastor Bowl had chosen on a trial basis. So the music committee bought a more expensive synthesizer, and even ended up paying the other company "rent" for having their keyboard on site for so long.

Meanwhile, Sandra Dodge originally had been hired as a visitation minister. She had good people skills, and most interviewees said she did a very good job visiting the sick and elderly. "Our elderly still miss her," one member said. However, under Pastor Bowl she began to function as an assistant minister by taking over much of the Christian education emphasis, by preaching regularly, and by taking over leadership of the contemporary service. Then, some people began to complain because Peter had promoted her when they felt she was unqualified for these greater responsibilities: she had little experience and did not have a college or seminary degree. Apparently, a larger salary went with her increased responsibilities. One member captured what several said: "She wasn't totally equipped to do all of these things. She got in over her head." Of course, another source of the complaints was her support for the contemporary service. "We had a pretty traditional membership base," another said. "The members were used to Established United Methodist Church and the way things had been run for 30 years, and this young person, Dodge, came in and started making changes. It just didn't sit well with people."

Connected with the complaints over the contemporary service was a battle over the pastors' changing the times of the worship services. Members questioned whether the pastors had gone through the proper channels to change the times. Apparently they had, and the change was approved at a congregational meeting, but from the perspective of many congregants the times changed suddenly and without warning on February 14, 1999. Services had been scheduled at eight A.M. and 10:10 A.M., with Sunday school at nine A.M. Now they had a nine A.M. traditional worship service, 11 A.M. contemporary worship, and Sunday school at 10 A.M. The move upset many, including the Sunday school teachers. Now the Christian education department was unhappy.

Open communication had clearly broken down. Members started to form cliques, and rumors abounded. One interviewee suggested that some members had manipulated people "to get them on certain committees so they knew what the outcome would be." One interviewee said that a group of dissatisfied people went to the pastor-parish relations committee and did not get anywhere. "A few went to the district superintendent, to no avail. Some went to Peter himself and tried to talk to him. That didn't work," he said. So, a petition was started, and eventually the dissidents obtained 120 signatures that a few members then took to the bishop asking for the removal of the pastors. During this stressful period, Peter's health began to suffer, and at the annual conference when the bishop announced pastoral appointments, Peter and Sandra were not reappointed to Established. Peter retired, and Sandra went back to college.

The interviewees expressed different assessments as to why the situation deteriorated to the point that members circulated a petition. One member said that Peter and Sandra had the best interests of the future of the church in mind when they introduced the contemporary service, but had difficulty communicating their vision. "They looked at the church and where the membership was going and assessed [that] the church was dying," this member said. "They made decisions to change a lot to help us stop dying and started the leadership team. They met and discussed every week and developed courses of actions but did not get the broad base of information from the congregation." This interviewee continued that Peter and Sandra couldn't get the people involved, "but they acted anyway."

Furthermore, it's clear that two powerful groups in the church were particularly upset with these pastors: One was the music committee and those involved in the traditional music program of the church, and the other a church group called the Middies. The Middies consisted of 60 to 80 longtime members, mostly retirees, including many who had money and long-term power in the church. Interviewees pointed out that not all the Middies were actively opposed to Peter and Sandra, but certain individuals within that group were. Some interviewees described them as complainers who didn't want any changes.

How extensive and how deep was this split in the church? "I wouldn't be surprised if the so-called troublemakers were only from about six to 10 members," said one interviewee. "We have just a few that are never happy." However, another member observed: "We have a bunch of street fighters here. They fight dirty. That is a reflection of our congregation." Age also figured as a factor, this member said. "Half of the members are 75 to 80. If it is at all different, people don't like it. People my age are very set in their ways, and so are the elderly." Many members, while agreeing that the match between Pastor Bowl and Established was not good, were appalled that a petition was circulated and given to the bishop. Three interviewees, in what I interpreted was not scapegoating, said that if the district superintendent had stepped in, things might not have reached the petition level. "He was too close with Sandra and Peter, and he couldn't be very objective. He should have taken a closer look at the congregation and maybe randomly talked to some members."

In the aftermath of the conflict, the petition, and the bishop's decision not to reappoint the two pastors, the bishop named two specially trained intentional interim ministers. However, before turning to the story of their leadership at Established, we need to look at the longer history of the church, and the town of which it is a part.

Background

The largest United Methodist church in the county, Established is located in the county seat—the county's largest community. It also sits in the Midwest's "tornado alley." One important event in the life of the congregation occurred in 1968, when a devastating tornado swept through and destroyed the entire downtown section. In its path, the twister destroyed every church within town limits, except one. (The members amusingly point out that whereas all the churches but one were destroyed, not one tavern was razed!)

Two United Methodist downtown churches were destroyed. The German United Methodist church, Central, was made up primarily of farmers and blue-collar workers from the area. The other congregation, somewhat larger, was the Methodist Episcopal church, First, and drew a greater percentage of professionals and white-collar workers. Both congregations were large enough to support their own full-time minister.

At the direction of the bishop, the state annual conference required the two churches to merge, which meant building one church building and forming one congregation. According to members who were part of the predecessor churches, votes taken in each congregation showed that First favored the merger, but Central adamantly opposed it. Opposition was raised not only because the congregations were so different, but also because of financial issues. Central felt its congregation had a much larger financial base than First. (Others, from First, maintained that the two congregations were actually quite evenly matched in financial resources—including their insurance settlements after the tornado.) The impasse was finally bridged when First voted to disband. The members joined Central and then swayed the votes to become one merged congregation! It was three or four years before the merged congregation decided it was unfair to carry on the name of only one of the predecessor churches and a new name, Established, was chosen.

When the tornado leveled the downtown, some church and community leaders, including leaders from First Church, envisioned an ecumenical church building complex to serve the denominations represented there. Such an endeavor fit the religious climate of the United States at that time, when many denominations considered consolidation. Within this religious climate, some interchurch faith centers were built in various sections of the country. (For example, such a center was built in the then newly planned city, Columbia, Maryland, halfway between Washington, D.C., and Baltimore.) "After the tornado we thought it was a good time to move the ecumenical thing along," one member recalled. "We had a planner come in and design an ecumenical church center. Every church was very gung-ho except Central Methodist. We ran into politics, and it killed the idea."

Nevertheless, some of this ecumenical endeavor found its way into the architecture of the new church. No expense was spared in the new complex. It was planned for use seven days a week for a myriad of purposes, not just by the congregation but also by the community. For example, choir concerts could be held there and, in fact, for years the high school held its concerts at Established because it was (and is) the nicest facility in town. Plays were staged there, and community groups from Alcoholics Anonymous to the Boy Scouts used the building. With the kitchen and fellowship hall, many banquets could be accommodated. Many outside groups have used the church in the years since it was finished. Although I never saw them, both a book and a video were produced to portray the remarkable architecture of the church.

Significantly, this magnificent structure was built debt-free. The city wanted both former properties for its redesign of the downtown. "The city bought both sites and said we could not have them back," one member said. Between the insurance money from both churches and a little from the town, the congregation never had to dig into its own pockets and sacrifice to build the church. Moreover, endowment funds accumulated quickly, so that by the middle of 2000, the endowment stood at $1.2 million. (By the time I made my research visit in fall 2001, because of the decline in the stock market, the endowment size had decreased but was still about $1 million.)

The union caused some defections. "We lost members from each congregation who said there was no way they would merge," said a member. Furthermore, after the merger the former members of Central tended to go to the early service and First people to the late. The vote on a new name for the church posed problems. "That was the hardest time." Other longtime members suggested that divisions arose when the church was being built. "There were some real complainers."

Today, older members claim the divisions stem back to the forced merger more than 33 years ago. Certainly, people continue to talk about the effect of the merger. According to a couple who are more recent members, "When we first came across the conflict, we were told that it was a 40-year-old thing and that it was now buried. I don't think that is totally right. There is a handful of people that seem to want things their way, and they have been in charge in the past." To be sure, all members who came from a predecessor church remain conscious from which church they came (and mentioned it to me). However, the intentional interim pastors think the merger conflict had matured into more a living memory than a primary cause for the conflict today. I'm inclined to agree. Just as a number of people left the church because of the forced merger in 1968, so also, during the conflict with the last pastors (1996–1999), "a whole layer of younger families left the church." In the aftermath of the petition, the bishop wisely appointed intentional interim ministers to lead the congregation in working through this most recent crisis.

While the recent crisis was acute and the conflict bitter, another factor beyond the church's control helped fuel the decline and the loss of younger members. The town had gone from a bustling population of about 12,000, when the churches were forced to merge, to a 2001 population of about 7500. This decline affected the whole county, as one large employer closed down its plant and another reduced operations and moved top management elsewhere. "I was the junior high librarian from 1964 to 1985," recalls one member. "I used to plan on 850 students. I don't think we even have 525 now. The county seems to be catering to the elderly. We don't have enough industry for workers. We have elderly and group homes." Others expressed similar sentiments. "Our children are in Texas and Oregon," lamented one couple. In these last 30 years, Established has declined from 1200 strong to about 800, with 335 giving units and an average worship attendance around 230. Though the whole county is in decline, Established members are concerned because other churches are growing while Established—once "the" church in town—is shrinking. "There are several churches in this community that have a high level of energy. I think we are losing numbers to them." According to several members, the Lutheran (ELCA) church is seeing growth, especially because of its dynamic youth program. The demographic projections for the next decade point to continued gradual decline in this county.

Intentional Interim Ministers

"These two pastors have a style and a very specific agenda," one member said, explaining that the pair laid out these ideas and said, "This is what we want at the end of three years." The senior intentional interim, Judy Moderator, described the task in broad categories of time. "The first segment is listening; the second is stabilizing; and then there is the leaving. There seems to be a God-given pattern of how things work."

One interviewee said the interims came in with a different attitude. "They talk about issues. They don't sweep them under the rug." Still another put their impact this way:

> They complement each other well. They have education backgrounds and that shows. They have been good for the congregation. So many people had negative attitudes, and now that they have been here awhile, people have responded well. If they say they will do something, they follow through on it. They have an effect on the younger generation. They make themselves available to you.

Who are these intentional interims and what qualifications do they bring to their positions?

Judy Moderator, the senior intentional interim minister, is clear about her call: "My passion in ministry is to develop the concept of the intentional interim in United Methodist terms, specifically to craft and refine the clergy team approach to interim ministry." Interestingly, the lifelong midwesterner came to her ministry in a roundabout way. Judy earned a bachelor's degree in speech and two master's degrees: one in counseling and the other in administration. After a few years as a high school teacher and counselor, Judy spent the next 33 years as a specialist in ministry, with much of that time at the request of the Metropolitan Commission as the director of a counseling and consulting office for area United Methodist churches. The Metropolitan Commission was a formal organization of Methodist churches and pastors in a larger population area, organized to do more in the area than any individual congregation or pastor could do. Judy specialized in conflict intervention ministry. She was an ordained deacon in full connection who had attended licensing school and was licensed as a local pastor. Before Established, Judy had served two intentional interim posts: an open-country, rural church with 200 members (1992–1996) and a blue-collar-town congregation of 400 members (1996–1999). She holds credentials and accreditation through the Intentional Ministry Network.

Marge Verve, intentional interim associate pastor, has a similar background as a lifelong midwesterner, similar varied work histories and similar clarity of vision. "I bring a background as a professional educator to the vocation of clergy." Marge earned two bachelor's degrees 23 years apart—the first with a business major and the second in mathematics. Shortly after earning the second degree, she received her master's degree in math. She worked in business for several years before she became a math teacher, first in high school and then at the college level for 13 years prior to 1999. Along the way she became a certified lay speaker in 1994 and obtained a license as a local pastor in 1997. After taking courses for licensing as a local pastor in the mid-1990s, she began interim ministry training in 1999. Before the interim ministry, she had been the local pastor of a small, rural United Methodist congregation from 1996 to 1999.

Most of the interviewees agreed that Established really needed the intentional interims. "This was a troubled church," said one member. "The animosity was very strong at the end of Sandra's and Peter's ministry." Another congregant said that the church needed strong leadership, and the two ministers fit the need. "They said this is how it is and how it is going to be." Yet, another said the intentional interims were necessary. "We needed to start from scratch," the member said. "One of the things Pastor Moderator wanted to do was teach us to teach ourselves to become a church that works together."

Some grasped how well they worked as a team. "They talk things over and discuss them," one member said. "They make decisions together. Pastor Moderator has the final word. They are very personable." Members immediately appreciated that the pastors would not tolerate gossip. On that first Sunday, according to one member, Pastor Moderator said, "My door is always open." The member commented, "There were no rumors. They wanted everything out in the open. They had committee meetings, and if there was a problem we'd address it. If there were an issue on the agenda that was sort of touchy, they wouldn't wait until the next month. They jumped right in and took care of it. In the past, [the pastors] pushed it out of the way and put it off." The spouse of this interviewee added, "That has made some people upset. They think the interims are too pushy. They need to get over that and give them a chance. We need to be pushed."

As I listened to the members talk, it became obvious that these two pastors had accomplished a lot in two years. One outsider gave this view of Established when the two arrived: "Members of Established are wealthy but acting poor. They aren't listening to each other. There are no programs happening. They are in a survival mode—anger is contagious and they had lost their vision."

The pastors immediately brought order out of chaos. "If you deal with a chaotic situation, you can't heal. We understand and are strong with the 2000 *Discipline* and how it works," said Pastor Moderator, referring to the 2000 United Methodist *Book of Discipline*, revised every four years. "There is no dealing under the table. If you want to know something, just ask," Pastor Moderator said. The interviewees commented on the pastors' gifts. "Pastor Moderator listens well; she communicates well; she has the skills of a counselor," a member said. "She gives good sermons. Her people skills are very strong. She is organized." One female member was impressed: "She is just a cool, smooth gal. I'm sure she gets flustered, but it would take quite a bit for her to show frustration in front of people. She knows how to handle whatever comes to us."

One member validated Pastor Verve's self-description. "The way she approaches her congregation is that of a school teacher," he said. Another congregant said Pastor Verve was a compassionate and emotional person, and several mentioned that she was "bubbly and that was good for the congregation." Several people noted how the pastors balance one another. One person summarized it this way:

> I think Judy Moderator is the right person for this job. She has been very good. She is very calming and soothing and her leadership is respectful. She is very complex, but listens very well to people. She is very mature and sensitive and she expects a level of responsibility from the people of the church. You don't feel you are being told to do something, but requests are couched in a way that you would do it for your mother. They are both very intelligent people. They each have a vision and stick to it. Verve sees it as more of a task and wants to get to the end goal. She is a little more demanding when she sees how something should be done. Its kind of like Verve is dad and Moderator is mom.

After about six months of listening, the pastors started to build a structure. "We scheduled the committees to meet on a monthly basis and gave the instructions about how to run these meetings. They now have the meetings at the same time of every month and know that they have to plan this every year." That is, the interims started an annual all-committee training session in January 2000 that included for each committee:

1. What is our disciplinary responsibility?
2. Where have we been?
3. Where are we going?

In answering the questions, committee members were to use as their plumb line the denominational goal to "Make Disciples of Jesus Christ."

A second of success was working with the youth, a task for which Pastor Verve assumed primary responsibility. She chose an administrative leadership style so that church members would actually lead the youth. First, the leaders began a new after-school program for mentoring younger kids, the "Wednesday School," complete with a light supper. Second, they reinvigorated the Sunday school. "Our numbers have really grown over the past two years," according to the Sunday school superintendent. "We tell students to bring a friend." Although they are having trouble finding enough teachers, Sunday school is on the upswing.

Third, Pastor Moderator took responsibility for confirmation training and new-member training. She strengthened confirmation by matching students with adult mentors who sit with students in class and help them with assignments between classes. Fourth, the youth group has reawakened. "We have the strongest youth now that we have had for several years," said one member. "We have some strong leaders among them." A high point for youth and adults alike came with a weeklong work trip during summer 2001 that they (13 youth, seven adults, two pastors) made to a mountainous rural area of Appalachia to repair homes of impoverished families. Another work trip was scheduled for summer 2002. Finally, both pastors have worked to bring younger families to the church with, among other things, a monthly Saturday contemporary service called the FROG Pond (Fully Rely On God). Attendance ranged from 35 to 82 people. In fall 2001 the congregation received (from financial gifts by a few members in the congregation) a new state-of-the-art media center for the sanctuary— three mounted cameras, a dedicated computer scanner, CD burner, other equipment, and a large screen. Though this kind of system can stir up resistance in a congregation, little opposition emerged at Established because a more "primitive" version had been planned with the original design of the church in the early 1970s. Thus, the sanctuary project of 1968–72 was completed in 2001.

The pastors also made some inroads into financial stewardship. Established has had trouble reaching its budget for the last several years. Some interviewees pointed out that the wealthiest people and the best financial givers were on fixed incomes and some of them were dying off. However, others recognized that because the church building was debt-free and the congregation well endowed, many members had not been taught to give at a sacrificial level. "It is sort of like kids that have been given everything," said one member. His spouse added, "The giving is not great. It is more like renter versus owner." Another had a slightly different perspective: "It wasn't our custom to tithe. I think Established has depended on people with the larger incomes to take care of the church. The middle and the lower classes don't give much at all." Nevertheless, the two intentional interims have led the congregation to give more. "Our giving is up 10 percent this past year," said a leader in the financial area. "We are hoping to increase further the level of giving. I give credit to these two interim pastors for the increase."

One congregational leader wondered whether—and how—the congregation would pay for staff it needs. "A church our size really needs two pastors," the member said. "The majority of the people may be thinking we can't afford two pastors. I think we can afford two pastors if we start building more from the community and more people give more money."

Several interviewees commented on the pastors' ability to motivate members. "They have involved many more laypeople in everything that is done," said one member. "We don't get the old stand-bys to do everything. They involved a wide range of people." Another member said this effort has caused grumbling among some congregants who think that with two pastors, the pastors themselves should do more of the work. The same member, however, understood that by delegating to the people, the interims were empowering the laity for ministry and developing a better base for positive ministry for the next pastor. Including people in decision making "has helped them feel more a part of things. They have led us, but they let us make decisions," said a member who characterized Judy Moderator as an expert at delegation. "She can make people do things without them actually knowing they are doing it," the member said. "She is very convincing. She understands people's psychology. She can handle confrontations and end up the conversation beings friends and happy." Another interviewee expressed it similarly: "Judy's personality is one of her biggest assets. When she looks at you and smiles, you know she means it. It's hard to say no to her. People do things when she asks them to. She can get people involved."

The intentional interims instituted a new committee they called the "Dream Team." In 2000 the General Conference of the United Methodist church changed the local-church organizational pattern, shifting from an administrative board and a council on ministries, each with committees under them, to a church council with committees under it. In a way the Dream Team is similar to the council on ministries, but with this crucial difference. With the Dream Team, the focus is not so much on programming as it is on envisioning for the future.

Issues about Intentional Interims

One interviewee who was positive about the intentional interims nevertheless complained about their titles. "It is always spelled out *intentional* interim pastor. They even put that in the bulletin." To him, the name conveyed a negative image, suggesting that the church was in more trouble than it was. While his concern might have been isolated, two widespread complaints surfaced, the first about cost. "We wanted one person because of finances, but ended up with two," one member said. "Financial difficulties have continued." While appreciating the work of both women, several interviewees felt that the senior interim minister, Judy Moderator, could have done the work herself. Some interviewees felt the two women were needed, but still lamented the cost.

Other members complained that the two pastors worked so closely that their style hurt efficiency. "You can't separate them," one member said. "We are getting only one and a half pastors for the price of two. They took vacations at the same time. They leave for meetings at the same time. They do things at the same time, the same way all of the time." Several suggested the two jointly attended too many conferences for intentional interims. Many believed only one should go at a time, leaving the other to handle things at church, especially on Sundays.

The pastors defended their actions. "We have been intentional about being together," said Judy Moderator. " We both wanted all of the information all of the time. There was such a triangle of information going around that we both wanted to get it at the same time. We actually got more out of the meetings. It is hard to get ahead of us, but impossible to get between us." The vacation they took at the same time had been planned before they arrived at Established. Because intentional interim ministry is specialized and needs special training, both pastors recognize the importance of conferences. In fact, the two interims did have separately defined responsibilities: Pastor Moderator was to work with the administrative committees—board of trustees, church council, staff-parish relations, lay leadership (nominations and personnel), finance, and stewardship. Pastor Verve was to work with the program committees, such as education, music, and evangelism, and with such programming as youth.

The final issue was whether Established needed to have an intentional interim arrangement for three years. "I think we could have accomplished what we need to in less than three years," said one member. But he acknowledged, "It has been good. I think it has been more of a wake-up call than anything. We had an outside source come in and say, 'You guys are in trouble.'" Another person said simply, "I think the members know what they want now. They want to move on. Three years may be too long." Several interviewees suggested that two years would have sufficed. Three or four believed the temporary nature of the arrangement depressed the level of commitment from the members. Another interviewee suggested that because intentional interims need to be focused on the crisis and turning things around, they could not focus also on all the normal needs. The congregation was definitely looking forward to a pastor who would stay for longer than three years.

Both Judy Moderator and Marge Verve struggled with the question of the length of stay—and scope of mission. They asked themselves, "Is it just our ministry to get them to stop yelling at each other and then bring the next person in to take over? Or should we continue to teach them more to get more pieces in place before you bring in the next person?" They also asked: When is the congregation ready to move forward? "If you only stay two years, you have to be sure at 18 months that they are where they need to be [to be] prepared for the next person," said Judy Moderator. "I think this congregation would have been OK after two years, but at 18 months we weren't positive they would be." The two pastors concluded that the third year could be profitable for Established if the leaders use it wisely. However, both pastors acknowledged that they have learned from the experience. "I am comfortable suggesting a two-year intentional interim—

say, in churches with conflicted situations—but time will tell what the magic numbers will be. So for the present, the length of the interim stay is still experimental."

Future

"The church is healthy, but needs to feel healthy," Judy said. This summarizes the situation at Established very well. Most of the people I talked to were eager to move on, confident that they were essentially a healthy congregation with a few chronic whiners and complainers who would not be a major obstacle to ministry. The intentional interims also saw the church as a loving, giving, faithful people with a few strong people who would perhaps never be happy. "I feel everyone is working in the same direction now," said one member. "Some people are always complainers. I personally haven't heard much of it lately. I don't think the complainers have any power."

But Judy and Marge also said the people had to "feel healthy," and a few interviewees were not so sure. "The group who were part of the petition to oust Pastors Bowl and Dodge has cooled down and smoothed things over. I don't feel they were reprimanded correctly," said one member. "What will stop them from doing this again?" For another, the Genesis story of Cain and Abel fits the church. At Established, brothers and sisters were fighting with one another and had been doing so since the forced merger over 30 years ago.

It is clear that the leadership quality of the next pastor will be key, but I know of very few congregations where leadership is not a crucial factor. The people of Established realize that if they want a younger, dynamic pastor, they will have to pay a much larger salary than they have in the past. The leadership of the congregation is now committed to do that. Most of the interviewees said that with a higher salary they could afford only one pastor, but many also said that in addition they would try for a youth director, at least as a part-time position. The chair of the church council believed they could afford two pastors and that a congregation the size of Established needed two. At the time of my research, no decision about staffing had been made.

It is encouraging for Established that United Methodism places a priority on making pastoral appointments. Generally, the larger-salaried positions are assigned first, and other situations follow. However, before that more customary path is taken, the bishop and his or her cabinet intend to address special-needs cases, some clergy-centered (for example, the need to place clergy couples in close proximity to one another) and others congregation-centered. As a follow-up to the intentional interim team, Established will be one of the first whose appointment needs are addressed. The interims said that the bishop and cabinet *will* assign a good pastor early in the process. Of course, whether the pastor Established receives will be a young man with a wife and small children, which is the church's dream-wish ideal for the next pastor, remains to be seen. The availability of the "perfect" pastor (as defined by several interviewees) at Established remained a big issue when my research there was completed.

Chapter 5

Majestic Episcopal Church
Northeast

A congregation's history can serve as a millstone around the church's neck or a heritage that enlivens the people for present ministry. In one congregation, the people live in the glorious past and do not understand why it can no longer be like "the good old days." In another, members celebrate the church's heritage and its connection to them, but their focus is on present and future mission. Majestic Episcopal Church falls between these two extremes, but in recent years has taken strides to look ahead.

There is no question about the glorious history of Majestic. In the late 1700s, a prominent doctor from a major East coast city, John Poet, bought and established an estate in the country about 90 miles from the city. He and several others laid plans to establish an Episcopal church in the tiny community, but John died before it came about. The doctor's son, Samuel, himself a prominent doctor, took up the cause. Samuel's daughter, in turn, married a new deacon of the Episcopal Church, John Victor, himself the son of a prominent merchant in the city. Samuel Poet and his son-in-law built a church on the family estate. Needless to say, John Victor became its first minister. He counted among his parishioners many nationally prominent families in the intellectual and political life of the time. After eight years as rector, John Victor was called to become a professor at a major East Coast university, where he stayed for almost 50 years.

As the congregation flourished, in 1832 a rector who was wealthy built, on his own property (a half mile from the church), a building for a children's school. He gave the school and the property to the church when he resigned. This building would play a significant part in the history of Majestic by functioning as a Sunday school, a guild room, and a free reading room and circulating library for the community. The building became known as the reading room, a designation that continues today. Then in 1857,

Majestic built a chapel connected to the reading room, and the church worshiped there during the winters for almost a century until 1955, when the main church building had central heating installed. Even after 1955, the eight A.M. service was held in the chapel until 1998, when the present rector and members moved it to the main church building.

In 1839, the original church building was torn down because it was structurally unsound, and services were held in the rectory (the rector's residence). In 1844, the congregation built a new church, an outstanding example of the Gothic Revival design in America. Today, the building, with its black walnut ceiling and open-timbered roof support, is one of the finest specimens of that discipline in America.

In the 20th century, a lifelong member of this congregation and its chief warden (lay president) for many years was elected president of the United States. Because of his prominence, two pictures hanging in the parish house capture the visitor's attention. The first shows the president and first lady, the king and queen of England, the prime minister of Canada, and other dignitaries after worship at Majestic. The second picture, at the funeral of the late president's wife, shows four U.S. presidents and families..

Finally, in 1956, Majestic received a sizable endowment of $250,000, which enabled it to build a parish house containing an auditorium with a stage, a kitchen, a formal sitting room, three parish offices, a nursery-school classroom, a choir rehearsal hall, and eight classrooms. A new rectory was finished in 1959.

Certainly Majestic has an awesome and distinguished history. This chapter will explore, among other questions, to what degree such a history has been a help or hindrance to the congregation in its present situation. However, the crises that rocked the congregation in the past two decades were not directly related to its history.

The Crises

Within the last 20 years, Majestic Church has asked two of its clergy leaders to resign. The conflict and pain surrounding these terminations played on the minds and emotions of the members. "We were wondering if we were the problem," one member said. "We had been through so much; we thought maybe we were causing it." The first crisis struck unexpectedly, occurring near the end of an 18-year pastorate. The Rev. Francis Magus arrived in

1966 as assistant to a beloved rector, John Silvan, who had been at Majestic since the end of World War II. Francis arrived at a time of high spirits in the congregation. When I visited there, Father Silvan was still the "ideal" pastor against whom all subsequent pastors have been compared.

Francis was young and had a winsome personality. He was dynamic, outgoing, and energetic, and was possessed of considerable personal charisma. Among other accomplishments, the youth group flourished under his leadership. One interviewee, who was a high school sophomore when Francis arrived, said the pastor made an impression: "He was a lot more liberal than our parents were." Others said Francis was knowledgeable about the Bible and the world, and was a great teacher. Given his wonderful leadership traits, Francis was called as rector when Father John Silvan retired. In the early years, the church continued to grow to the point that the congregation had two pastoral assistants.

Then sometime in the late 1970s, fortunes began to reverse. The people I interviewed who were there at the time identified a changed attitude in Francis when he returned from National Guard duty one summer. After that, members perceived that his leadership waned; his investment in Majestic shifted. He also went through a divorce, and many members of Majestic were not pleased about the way he handled the aftermath. The relationship between Francis and the congregation continued to deteriorate until leaders of Majestic approached the diocese. By 1984, a severance package had been worked out, and Francis prepared to leave.

Just at that moment, a devastating fire of suspicious origin gutted the beautiful historic 1844 church. Francis Magus offered to stay to help the congregation through the crisis, but the leadership felt that arrangements for his leaving had been completed and that both parties should follow through with them. Majestic found itself in extreme crisis without pastoral leadership. Fortunately, in January 1985, the diocese appointed an interim rector, the Rev. Robert Bond. Interviewees who were members then reported that he was able to calm the congregation and heal many wounds. Members loved him. He also led the project to rebuild the church after the fire.

The fire played significantly in Majestic's reversal of fortunes, made even worse by depressing conditions within the church and in the wider area. First, by 1984 membership and participation in the congregation had decreased considerably and the *esprit de corps* was poor. Second, the largest employer in the area began "downsizing," and many middle-management people were either transferred or let go (and then moved because of a new job). Amid this recession, members faced whether to rebuild the church building. A strong element in the congregation wanted to replicate the church exactly as it was before the fire. However the church was underinsured, so when the congregation decided to rebuild, it could be only with modern materials. An outside organization did the fund raising, and congregational leaders urged giving to the building fund. With the double emphasis, Majestic survived this crisis.

On the plus side, the congregation had preserved the remarkable 1844 building—so striking that a wonderful photograph of the church dominates the main page of Majestic's Web site. However, the church building stands independent from the offices and the Christian education building, with a parking lot between (allowing members a perfect excuse to go to their cars rather than moving to the Christian education building for Sunday school). Moreover, not only does the church have to be heated separately, but also there are no restrooms!

In my mind, there was also a danger in restoring the church exactly as it was. In the last two-thirds of a century, Majestic had partially succumbed to becoming a museum to its past, especially to the days when the U.S. president and his family had been such prominent leaders. The congregation was somewhat "shackled" by its history. The present rector doesn't think that is still the case, in part because almost all of the members who could remember the glory days are dead. Also, it is significant that before the fire, plaques displayed throughout the church depicted its history. After the fire, most of the plaques were removed. A few remain, primarily those connected with the U.S. president. From my interviews with members in 2001, I became convinced that Majestic honored the "glory days of the past" but members could focus on the present congregation and its present and future needs. Father Robert Bond, who had brought significant healing to the congregation, stayed until May 1986, when a new rector, the Rev. Martin Abbot, was called. At that point, Father Bond entered his planned retirement.

Majestic had called Martin Abbot with the encouragement of the diocesan staff, but several interviewees said the match never should have been made. Majestic was not the congregation Martin Abbot expected, and he was not the church leader they needed. "He is a kind person, very spiritual, but not a people person and not an administrator," one person remarked. A few said Martin would have been suited to life in a monastery.

Two characteristics seem to have grated on members the most. First, several interviewees thought he was inflexible and had trouble with dissension concerning his decisions. Two members even noted that he actually had left a few meetings when the tensions rose. "Father Martin was more into the 'I'm the priest; this is my church, and this is how it will happen,'" said a supporter who left for a while after Martin was dismissed.

The view of Father Martin's inflexibility extended to the worship service. "He was a caring, loving person, but when he put the robes on, something happened to him," said one person. He was rigid in his worship leadership, said another: "If you made a mistake, it was a major crisis." The altar guild was on pins and needles that it might do something wrong.

Secondly, members said Martin was an extreme introvert, shy and withdrawn. Most especially, many said he was not inviting to children—not wanting, for example, any disruptions in the worship service. Moreover, interviewees suggested that he was not helped by a parish administrator who had a strong personality, or by dissension within the music program. On the other hand, many suggested he was faithful and good in visiting the sick, the shut-ins, the dying, and the bereaved, and that he was a good preacher. One supporter said that Martin was "a good person in the wrong place."

During his tenure attendance plummeted, and budgets problems grew, and it was hard to find enough members willing to fill out the vestry. Martin lost energy as he realized that his dreams for ministry there would not be realized. While the vestry tried to work with Martin over these difficulties, a group of members bypassed the vestry by writing to the bishop about Martin. At the same time, some members who attended only on Sunday were hardly aware that serious problems existed. Communication with the congregation had become a serious issue.

The bishop assigned a skilled assistant, the Rev. Jonah Ford, to work with the rector and the congregation on these issues. Jonah Ford held monthly meetings with the congregation, and saw that the whole conflict was laid out on the table. What surprised members of the vestry was "that the parish was as aware of the dysfunction as they were." After listening to the people, Jonah Ford also worked with Martin on a settlement for him to leave Majestic. Separate from the vestry, an ad hoc group was formed to sift through the conflict and help Martin to move on with dignity.

By the time Martin left in March 1995, attendance at the late service had dwindled to between 30 and 40 people with an additional 25 to 30 at the eight A.M. service. Sunday school had diminished to the point that Martin was sometimes the only person there. Nevertheless, some members really appreciated Martin's ministry and left the congregation when he was dismissed.

Majestic was at a critical juncture. "We were almost ready to close down," said one member. "The diocese worked very closely with us . . . and told us not to panic. . . . We were seriously worried about this church. The diocese told us it would be a lot of work, but we could rebuild ourselves by working on the strengths that were here and moving forward." Another member noted that unlike the departure of Francis Magus, Martin Abbot's leaving fell at a time when "the money was not coming in," and that latter crisis brought the congregation closer to closing.

Through the diocese, Jonah Ford worked with the congregation until Martin's tenure was finished. Then the bishop asked Majestic to hire a consultant, Bob Laity, a Roman Catholic layperson trained to work with parishes in conflict and to prepare for an interim minister. One of his tasks was to lead a self-study of the congregation. "Bob did a lot," said one member. "We had to end the conflict before we could move forward. We worked on establishing a policy of how to deal with conflict. We learned about triangulation. It was a lot of work to get us to not be in conflict with one another."

Jonah's and Bob's work brought both healing and some self-understanding of how Majestic had become so dysfunctional. However, the worship life of the congregation continued to suffer for several months between the departure of Father Abbot and the arrival of the Rev. Norm Competent, the intentional interim minister. Bob Laity was not present on Sunday mornings; so for several months' duration, a different guest minister led the worship each week. The lack of continuity proved a further hardship on the congregation.

Intentional Interim Minister

"God sent him to us. We were lost and he helped us find our way, in such a classy manner." The statement by a member echoed the sentiments of the majority of interviewees that the presence of Norman Competent, the intentional interim who served from November 1995 to March 1997, was absolutely essential for the health of the church. Without Father Competent, these members said, the church would not have been ready to respond positively to the ministry of the current rector.

Interviewees agreed that Father Competent knew the role of an interim, knew what Majestic needed and achieved it while making sure the people knew he and his wife would be leaving in a year or so. "If there was something we went to him for help with, if it wasn't something that the priest was to handle, he turned it back on us," said one member. "That was a different tactic for us." Another said, "He told us we could not become too dependent on him and he could never be our regular priest. He kept his boundaries and gave us what he thought we needed."

Majestic was Norman Competent's fourth intentional interim ministry assignment, so he brought experience to his ministry at Majestic. Moreover, his background had included working on two diocesan staffs for 20 years (1971–1991) as the diocesan deployment officer, a job that involved him closely with clergy as they moved from one parish to another and with the congregations during their vacancies. Because of his position, he became involved with the Interim Ministry Network and in the late 1980s conducted interim training for Episcopal pastors in his diocese. Father Competent also had special training in organizational development and in working with addictive organizations and addictive people.

Because of this background, many noted the skill level he brought to Majestic. "He didn't come to win a popularity contest; he came to do what the diocese wanted him to do," said one member. "You immediately took a liking to him. He would ask, 'Why are you doing this?' He seemed to know exactly what he was supposed to do here. . . . He did things in a nice way, but told us what we were doing wrong."

One interviewee described him as a computer whiz. He brought computers into the parish and updated the telephone system. He updated the personnel policies of the congregation, and put several policies in writing. He further noticed immediately that the grounds around the church looked neglected, that the rectory needed work, and that certain rooms in the parish house, like the kitchen, needed a thorough cleaning. Because Father Competent realized that how a congregation presents itself to others in its physical plant and grounds often reflects the self-image of the congregation, he worked with the members to clean up the buildings and grounds. One interviewee said that his emphasis in this area helped the congregation "get out of its funk."

In light of the "funk," it is instructive to look at Father Competent's first annual report, written less than two months after he had arrived.

He wrote, "I have been amazed by all the strengths I am observing among you." Then he commended members for doing so many things responsibly and competently in serving the community and strengthening the parish—by having a year-round emphasis on stewardship; by being warm, welcoming, kind, and supportive; by allowing the building to be used during the week for self-help groups, programs for babies and for seniors, Scouts, the food pantry, and the nursery school. He applauded them for rebuilding the staff in the past several months. Father Competent then turned to "Looking Ahead." "You value your heritage . . . and grow from the strengths of your past. . . . You are working hard at accepting the realities of the past, both disappointments and differences. . . . You are deepening your ways of working together, of accepting and appreciating each others' gifts, and of supporting one another mutually." He concluded, "You and God have been working together creatively and faithfully. God calls you forward. You are on the Way." This affirmation of the people at Majestic was exactly what they needed to hear at the time.

In his next year's report, he reaffirmed the strengths that he had enumerated a year earlier, but subsequently turned to the challenges that faced them: "continuing to bring new leadership on board, . . . completing elements of reorganizing the parish, . . . continuing to deepen mutual acceptance, appreciation, and encouragement, . . . believing and acting on the belief that you need, deserve, and are entitled to a good rector with maturity, balance, and poise in every area of his or her life, . . . and establishing your new pastoral relationship with the spiritual gifts of mutual trust, esteem, and caring." Interestingly, he described the difficulties Majestic had had in mutual acceptance, appreciation, and encouragement in the context not just of congregational difficulties but those of the wider community. "I see [deepening mutual acceptance] as a way through the contention of this region, contention born, I believe, of disappointment over the loss of estate owners, employers, transportation, and leaders—and for this parish, the disruption of two pastoral relationships." But he concluded his report with words of encouragement, "Be of good cheer in all this. God challenges you because you are worthy."

Parishioners described Father Competent as having "a very pastoral presence and a good sense of humor." He used these skills as he kept communication open in the parish by holding parish meetings to let everyone know what was going on and to bring people together to look toward the future rather than the past. "The most important thing he did was listen," said one member. "He listened to the problems and then threw questions back at us to make us look for our own solutions." Another member said he made people stick to issues rather than sidetracking. "He showed us how to make Majestic heal and grow. He told us to get a grip on things and take responsibility with our church. This is when people started to turn around. He made us focus." Another declared, "He had a lot of strength to bring the church community together but not in a demanding way."

Father Competent made subtle changes in the worship service so it was less rigid and somewhat more informal. One altar guild member said he helped by reminding them, "You are competent; use that competence and do what you need to do." The message helped relax them. "Everything was all right with him, even if there was a mistake. He never made you feel bad." Several members remember his helpful sermons.

Father Competent possessed great skills in the tasks that needed to be done, and yet he led in a way that, as one member put it, "was very calming." Another called him a peacemaker. "He listened more than he talked. He was a gentle man and urged us to take our time." His leadership created an atmosphere in which people who had been split over the previous pastor were able to come together and work together again. Before he left, Father Competent even prepared a congregational profile, which was given to all the prospective candidates for rector at Majestic and proved to be of tremendous help to the current rector.

The congregation did take its time in selecting its next rector, allowing six months between the leaving of Father Competent and the arrival of the current rector. "The vestry had formed, and we all liked each other and knew we could work together, and we weren't afraid to disagree with one another," said one member. In fact, the vestry knew the needs of the congregation so that it did not need to rush to take the first person it interviewed. "We knew we were healthy because we knew that if we interviewed the people and they weren't right, we would keep on going," said one member. The diocese encouraged the church, saying that the process would work. Meanwhile, the leaders kept the congregation fully informed by reporting each week on their progress. All in all the congregation had seen tremendous growth in what turned out to be the three years between the leaving of Martin Abbot and the arrival of the current rector.

The New Settled Pastorate

"I have waited for Chuck Gregarious all of my life," said one member, who expresses the popular opinion. "He does well in his own skin. He likes being a parish priest. He would stand for God against 40 lions. He is a man of God, but he listens to any person who talks to him. I could take anything to Chuck. He would be understanding no matter what it is." Members unanimously saw Chuck as both open to God (one member called him "full of the Holy Spirit") and open to people, with a deep sense of caring for the people of the congregation. Chuck also communicates well in one-on-one situations, in preaching, and in written presentations. In fact, since his arrival he has written a weekly column in the local newspaper about various aspects of the Christian faith. Having read several of these columns, I can testify that they were very insightful, interesting, and timely. In all these crucial areas, he was indeed the leader the congregation was looking for.

The Rev. Charles Gregarious is a Midwest native who received a bachelor's degree in German and journalism at a midwestern university. He received his master's degree in German in 1987. Then, he entered an Episcopal seminary in the East (1987–1990) and served as assistant pastor in an eastern congregation from 1990 to 1995. At that point he was called to a congregation in the South. Father Gregarious told me that he was not planning to come North, but his wife, who was from the area, saw the profile of Majestic and asked him to consider it; if the post did not work out, the family would at least have a visit with her mother. "I really wasn't interested in coming back up. To my surprise, they said, 'We want to interview you.' I saw the buildings and thought, there is no way I can come here. There was very little physically that attracted me. However, I came out of the interview knowing this is exactly where I needed to be, and this is where I wanted to be. I haven't had any doubts about it since."

Chuck Gregarious, with his wife and two young sons, began to serve Majestic on November 2, 1997. A few weeks later he wrote his first annual report, which, although brief, set the tone for his ministry. He wrote:

> I do think it is appropriate to lay out before you what I hope to accomplish in my first full year at Majestic—very little. That is to say, my primary focus for my first 12 months will be to get to know everyone in the parish. I hope, by the end of my first year, to know the name of every parishioner. This is because I believe

no work can be accomplished without the one underlying foundation of our very faith—love. Love is based on relationship, and relationship means knowing each other. If we don't know each other, doing any work, no matter how good and holy, will ring hollow.

But even in this annual report, Chuck could not keep from suggesting some areas in which he would like to concentrate: more youth involvement, a more developed Christian education program for adults as well as for children, a well-defined newcomer's program, and a far-reaching and hands-on outreach ministry. He said he was but dreaming out loud, but warned them that he encouraged dreaming.

In fact, many praised his ability to dream and experiment. "He brings the gift of a great imagination," said one member. "He is not afraid of new projects. He wants to try everything. He has the enthusiasm of an Alka-Seltzer. It is hard for him to contain what is in him that wants to come out." Another said he had a good attitude toward new projects. "We don't have to commit forever to these things, but we can try them. He has a real interactive relationship with the congregation."

So, during the first year, when he said he was going to originate "very little," he and the congregation actually innovated several things. He held quarterly meetings to keep communication open, but also led the congregation in defining a mission statement and creating action plans for the coming year. In these meetings he led the members in reducing the size of the vestry from 12 members to nine, a more manageable number for a congregation of this size. The Christian education people planned and carried out a Christmas pageant. Under outreach, he led the congregation in beginning an after-school reading program, while he took his turn in reading with youngsters from the town (a practice he continues). Most important, he handled the potentially divisive issue of closing the chapel, located a half-mile from the church. Discussions about the chapel's future had been taking place for some time before Chuck arrived. Closing the chapel would mean moving eight A.M. worship to the church—a hard call for many members. Knowing that a decision had to be reached, Chuck skillfully met with members and let them make the determination. "Chuck did a great job," said one member. "He handled the meetings well. He would call on people for their opinion." In the end, it was the members' decision to move worship to the church. "The people actually got up and said, 'It's time; we need to move out of the chapel and into the church,'" one member said. Finally, to continue to raise morale, Chuck saw that a pictorial directory of church members was produced.

Of course, new programs didn't end after the first year. Subsequently the congregation developed a Web site, for Epiphany introduced Taizé worship (a quiet service using silence and a distinctive style of brief, repetitive song that originated in the Taizé community in France), incorporated a children's sermon into worship, added a New Year's Eve service, erected a new large church sign in front of the church, began an adult Sunday school class, started three Bible study groups, initiated new hospitality events such as a young parents' group and a Christmas party, started a blood drive, participated in the CROP Walk, started a men's breakfast, and began a youth group. When Father Gregarious arrived, there were just three acolytes and no youth group; when I conducted my research, the church had 30 kids participating with 12 belonging to the youth group.

Weekly worship attendance rose, with an influx of more young people and young families, who are a match with the pastor and his young family. At the time of my visit, from 30 to 40 worshipers attended the early service, and from 60 to 80 the later one. Chuck showed himself to be an informal worship leader and, according to many interviewees, a very good preacher. On the Sunday I visited, I heard an excellent biblically based, contemporarily relevant sermon. The nursery during worship now had many children. The overall atmosphere, according to the members, was a friendly and open church with new leadership being brought unto the vestry and other key positions.

Mission Statement

One member said that the people have bought more into the pastor's vision in the last three years than in the 12 before Father Gregarious. Indeed, I discovered most people knew the motto that heads the mission statement: "To know Christ and to make him known." The people were less clear about what the mission statement said beyond the motto. The statement contained six specific areas in which "we believe that God's Holy Spirit will empower us to express this mission":

1. worship/spiritual nurture,
2. outreach,
3. youth,
4. Christian education,
5. pastoral care, and
6. hospitality/fellowship.

One member said that it was a good mission statement for a church many of whose congregational stalwarts have been around for so long. "They read this and don't see anything revolutionary," the member explained. "It is what they have been trying to do all along. What we tried to do in writing the mission statement was keep things very similar to what the older folks have been doing."

Three and a half years later, Father Chuck indicated that he wanted to expand the members' concept of evangelism. "That is not even in our mission statement at all. People didn't want to think about it. In the long run, I want to start training people and work on raising these people up to be evangelists."

Discussing other priority areas, Father Chuck said he wanted to work on Christian education. "The concept of adults being in Sunday school and children being in worship has never really been grasped here. We average about five [adults] in Sunday school." He had started three Bible studies (none of them on Sunday morning), and people were coming to them. Within five years, he wanted to see 10 Bible studies, many in people's homes. Second, he desired more emphasis on outreach. The after-school reading program had existed for three years, and it was going very well. The community children were responding to it, and the church had volunteers to help with it. Part of the need in outreach, according to Chuck, was to reaffirm the original purpose of the nursery school that met two and a half hours every weekday in the parish house and was begun as a ministry to the community.

Such glowing comments could give the impression that everything that Chuck and the congregation tried worked and was well received. Such is not the case, as can been seen in his annual reports. In the 1999 report, for example, Father Chuck observed:

> Over the course of our second year together, we have tried many new things. Some have encountered stumbling blocks or have proved to be things we do not want to do after all: the difficulty in

finding a new coordinator for the After School Program, the canceled Vacation Bible Camp and difficulty starting a Jr. Youth Group, and the Unified Committee Meeting Night (which after a trial period failed to gain much support and has now been discontinued).

The after-school program continued despite the difficulty in finding a coordinator, but in the annual report for 2000, Father Chuck had dismal news: "For the first time in three years we did not have a Christmas Pageant or Epiphany Party. We let go of the hope for a Vacation Bible School for last summer—again." He also expressed disappointment with committees. "If there is a shortcoming to be lamented this year, it is that with few exceptions our committees did not meet regularly." In the renewal of any parish, there will be many setbacks as well as successes. Majestic offers a concrete example of how uneven the pattern is even in a congregation full of growth, enthusiasm, and hope.

Early on in his ministry, Father Chuck faced the ongoing problem of Majestic's nursery school, which had its own staff and operated semi-independently from the congregation but was nonetheless a ministry of the church. When it started, the nursery school was to be a ministry to the whole area. School was in session for two and a half hours every weekday, but it did not function as a day care center. Over the years it had become a very good place for middle-class families who had a parent free during the day to bring and retrieve the children, but because it was not set up for all day, those with the fewest economic resources could not use it. With the support of the vestry, Father Chuck wanted the school to minister to those most in need in town. "The school has been the source of sleepless nights," he said. A board of church members (including those who worked at the school) had been considering whether and how to modify the school to serve the needy and perhaps even make it a day-care facility. Needless to say, several people did not want the school to change its focus. This issue was far from resolved when I conducted my interviews in June 2001.

Two members suggested that in areas important for mission, Chuck "likes to be in charge," and so occasionally "butts heads" with members who themselves want to be in charge. And a few members were simply sitting back, waiting to see what would happen with the new minister. However, more people were active in the congregation, buying into the vision and getting involved. "Church is not a spectator sport—you have to participate," said one member, reflecting on Father Chuck's mission. Another said, "To think you can become a Christian by going to church on Sunday is like trying to become a car by sleeping in the garage!"

Chuck himself said that leadership—"the willingness to pick up a ball and run with it"—was the biggest issue facing this congregation. He recognized that people's lives were insanely busy. "Lots of people have said to me, 'I will help, but I will not lead.' That is frustrating. I don't want to run things and have people follow my orders. That is a recipe for burnout and resentment." In today's culture, finding qualified people for leadership positions seems to be a perennial problem in most congregations, especially small congregations. However, one of the new members from a Roman Catholic background said, "One of the things that amazes me is that we get things done. We get them done with a small parish. We touch a lot of people and do a lot of things. We pull together to get things done."

In a loving context, members who knew how Chuck worked during the week laughingly acknowledged that he was disorganized. "Being a good preacher and being good with people don't require him to be organized," one member said. "I think the church had a sense they could take care of details. They wanted someone to help with their spiritual growth." Another member expressed it this way: "He is not really scatter-brained, but what happens is he has so much going on in his mind, he isn't organized. His strengths are that people love him; his sermons are wonderful; his advice is wonderful; he is very caring regardless of who you are." Only two interviewees seemed a little annoyed that he wasn't better organized. One suggested that because he isn't organized, he tends to micromanage, and the other added, "He loses everything." Nevertheless, the prevailing view was expressed in statements like these: "What draws me to him is his humility. I feel he is the truly most good person I have ever met. He really has the interest of other people in his heart. As I have gotten to know him, he has chinks in his armor like all people, but he is still a great person." Or another, "One of the vestry people said, 'He wears his skin well; he is not full of himself.' Chuck is absolutely not full of himself. He is not afraid to make a mistake. He feels so called to do what he is doing."

Future

"The future looks good here," said two influential and long-term members of the church in separate interviews. Almost everyone I interviewed said that the good future was connected with Chuck's continued leadership. "I hope Chuck will still be here in five to 10 years. We aren't going anywhere without him at the moment." Another member added that the congregation hopes that Chuck stays until his children go to college. "I don't see us growing rapidly, but more slowly."

Some interviewees acknowledged limits on how much change and growth would occur in the next five to 10 years. They expressed the need for a balance between change to bring in younger families, and yet not so much that older members would feel left out. One interviewee declared that "older people" is a mental issue, not an age issue, and that many of the long-term members welcomed change. "I think the people are wonderful here, but I am a little more toward younger music and worship that is not quite so formal," one member said. "The older congregation likes it the way it is. I don't want to step on anybody's toes. We are ready for a little change, but not to change too drastically that people want to leave. I would like to see more freedom and less formality." A couple suggested that keeping things in balance may require Chuck to move more slowly than he may wish. They also felt that the absence of restrooms in the church would hurt Majestic's growth. "Unless you revamp the church, he is really limited." Nevertheless, this couple was confident that, if Chuck continued to be their pastor, Majestic would continue growing and he would continue to bring younger people into membership.

In summary, the majority view was expressed by one member: "I see the church physically growing month to month. Over a year you look back and see new programs, new outreach, and new families. I think [Majestic] will continue to do this. . . . There is so much life in the church with young people and older people and kids."

Chapter 6

Peace Congregational Church
California

L ocated in a large metropolitan area in California, Peace Congregational Church has always seen itself as a sanctuary church. That is to say, throughout its history, this congregation has offered sanctuary from the ways of the world by being committed to nonviolence, inclusiveness, and respect for all human beings. A watchword for Peace, coined by an influential member 30 or 40 years ago, is "There is a light here." "There will be people drawn to the light here, which is acceptance," said one member. "We are not creedal, and we are not dogmatic. Everybody is on separate spiritual journeys, and that is OK with everyone else. We accept people where they are in their journey. We have agnostics, atheists, and Jewish people here," she continued. "Acceptance is not an easy concept. It is something everyone has to wrestle with. Peace will not grow like an evangelical church. The faith fostered here is like Jacob wrestling with God. It is a faith you have to wrestle with. It won't be superpopular but will be healthy and continue to grow."

A sociologist would describe Peace as a liberal, Protestant, urban, ethnically diverse small church that is politically active. However, this description fails to capture the passion with which the members understood this congregation. One interviewee saw it as being on "the road less traveled." Another suggested that "suffer all the children to come to me" might be an appropriate scriptural text for this congregation. "The doors of the church are open to all regardless of race, color, creed, sexual orientation, whatever." So what brought this congregation to the brink of closing?

The Crisis

One member said Peace was in crisis from 1989, when a well-liked pastor, the Rev. Penny Action (1985–89), left, until the calling of the present pastor, the Rev. Paul Proclaimer, in 1998. This member also said that the intentional interim minister, the Rev. Bee Love (1996–98), was essential in laying the foundation for a future filled with hope. However, the congregation's experience with interim ministers was not all positive. In 1989 an interim pastor had started to serve the church, but his ministry ended in crisis over whether he could or should become the permanent minister. When the Rev. John Independent (1990–1994) was subsequently called, expectations of the pastor and the congregation never matched. One member said, "He never identified with us or us with him." Many members felt that John wanted to focus on the social-action concerns of the metropolitan area at a time when the congregation was in decline. He was accused of never being in the office, of providing little congregational leadership except on Sunday mornings, and of being untrustworthy—having a secretive lifestyle and coping not very ably with unacknowledged personal problems. During his tenure members left, attendance at Sunday worship declined, and financial hardships arose.

The crisis came to a head when Peace sought to balance the budget by significantly reducing John's salary. With the ensuing conflict from this plan, the lay leadership asked United Church of Christ judicatory officials to intervene by bringing a consultation team to the congregation. It sent two specially trained pastors who worked with the congregation in early 1994. For two days in February 1994, the consultants met for one hour each with John, the church council, and groups of eight to 12 members and friends of the church. They met with a total of 45 people and received letters from three others. The 45 also filled out questionnaires identifying the issues of conflict and concern.

The report recommended that the council appoint a committee of eight—four who supported the pastor and four who wanted him to leave. The moderator of the congregation was to serve on the committee, as were the UCC consultants. Called the committee on pastoral relations, these selected people met and listed six issues to explore about John's ministry. After meeting with John and discussing the issues, the committee formulated several requirements for John's continuation as pastor of Peace. Finally, in June 1994 the pastoral relations committee recommended that

John Independent not continue as minister of Peace. The congregation concurred with the recommendation.

During this turmoil, the church's earlier history was exhumed. It became apparent that Peace had not yet put behind it a similar crisis that had occurred almost 30 years before. After the long tenure of a much beloved pastor, another pastor, the Rev. Henry Cause (1964–1969), was called, and during his pastorate the congregation's membership declined precipitously. According to a history of the congregation, Henry believed in "'creative ferment' [his phrase] in all departments of church life." His sermon series on "Christian Agnosticism" evoked great controversy. By 1968, Henry acknowledged domestic problems in his home but denied several rumors circulating about him. Nevertheless, according to the history: "Increased tensions and problems in the church revolving around dissatisfaction with governance, theological interpretations of Jesus, and other issues caused a major cleavage to occur within the membership." In February 1969, by congregational vote Henry's ministry at Peace was terminated. Hurt and upheaval preceded and followed the vote, with 30 members leaving the congregation. However, for the next 28 years the issues involved in Henry's dismissal were not discussed in the congregation, until, under the guidance of Bee, the intentional interim minister (1996–1998), they were brought into the open.

As a result of the 1990–94 crisis and the lingering effects of the earlier one, Peace had almost hit rock bottom by 1994. Once again, another part-time interim was appointed to the congregation, but this ministry also ended in controversy over whether she could be a candidate for the permanent position. By 1996, Peace was down to as few as 20 people in worship. "In the last 10 years I thought the congregation was going to go down the drain," one member said. "There were more people in the choir than in the congregation." An astute observer said, "There was a lot of anger; they were ready to give up; they put Band-Aids on the wounds instead of fixing them. Futureless would be the way I would describe it."

Background

The church was founded in 1905 in a recently incorporated community of fewer than 3,000 people. By 1910, the community itself was annexed into a large metropolitan city while keeping its own name. Within a couple of decades it mushroomed and became saturated in population by the 1950s. At the time of my visit, it was one of the few remaining neighborhoods in that city where people walked and shopped in small local stores. Residents walked in relative safety day or night, and lived in mostly lower-middle-class housing. The area had long had a diverse ethnic population with increases in recent years of Armenians and Latinos. In the last decade the neighborhood was beginning to attract young urban professionals.

Peace had 10 pastors in its first 13 years—including a United Brethren pastor from Greensburg, Pennsylvania. The non-Congregational pastor's call shows the denominational independence Peace has always exercised in calling its pastors. Peace began to flourish in 1918 when it called a Methodist Episcopal pastor, Dr. George Pacifist, who had been pastor of First Methodist Church in the community and district superintendent of the Methodist Episcopal Church for the entire city. When he became pastor of Peace, he brought one-third of the members of First Methodist with him. Unusual for World War I years, he was a pacifist. "He took seriously the commandment of Jesus to love your enemies, and could not sanction the church's support of war," according to the history. "The Methodist Church did not then uphold the pacifist position; consequently this man who followed his conscience was relieved of his duties."

Peace grew rapidly. Other churches—Lutheran, Baptist, Presbyterian, and Catholic—had not yet built in the community, and Peace church became the community church for that area, according to the history. Membership grew from 167 to 608, and the Sunday school had an average attendance of 385 by 1926. In October 1926, Dr. Pacifist resigned to become general secretary of the federation of churches for that area. However, he and his wife remained members and key leaders of this congregation for the rest of their lives and also key supporters of—and in many ways partners with— the successor, the Rev. Allan Everything, and his wife.

In 1996 when the intentional interim minister asked the congregation who was this congregation's angel, members quickly identified Allan Everything, the pastor from 1926 until 1963. He became the pastor, the one against whom everyone else would be judged by this congregation. After graduating from Princeton University in 1916, he went to Egypt to teach. Wartime experiences there convinced him of the "futility, waste, and wrong of war." He worked at a Syrian orphanage in Jerusalem under the Red Cross and in Near East relief. In 1919–20 he traveled through India and also studied social movements in China, Korea, and Japan. Back in America, he studied at Union Seminary and Columbia University in New York between 1921 and 1925. Ordained a Presbyterian minister in 1922, he served several congregations in the metropolitan area until receiving a master's degree in religious education from Columbia in 1925. Married in 1923, he and his wife spent September 1925 to June 1926 traveling throughout China working for world friendship through the Fellowship of Youth for Peace. Allan came back to the U.S. to be called as pastor of Peace in October 1926. The history does not record how he learned of the opening on the West Coast, but it seems likely that Dr. Pacifist would have heard about this kindred spirit, Allan, and might well have been instrumental in bringing him to the congregation. In fact, Allen and his wife were welcomed to the church at a reception that also honored George Pacifist and his wife. Allen's election began a pastoral relationship that would carry through the world depression, World War II, the development of the atomic bomb, the Korean War, and the beginning of civil unrest in the cities in the 1960s.

The congregation's view of Allan was captured by a longtime member: "With him you walked on air. He was so spiritual. . . . He was the most godlike man some people have ever known." With his worldwide contacts he brought famous speakers to the church: Dr. Toyohiko Kagawa, a Japanese social reformer, pacifist, and religious leader; Muriel and Doris Lester, known for their settlement house in London, Kingsley Hall; Dr. Martin Niemöller, World War I submarine commander who became a Lutheran pastor and was arrested for his opposition to the Nazis; Agnes Sandford, one of the pre-eminent spiritual healers of the 20th century; Norman Cousins, author, lecturer and longtime editor of the *Saturday Review*; and many others.

Peace reflected its pastor's activism, giving money beyond their regular benevolence to people caught in the Chinese Rice Bowl in the 1930s, to Mexican laborers being returned to their homes in Mexico, to Kagawa and his Japanese mission, to the Lesters and the London settlement house, to missionaries in India, and to many other people and places. As soon as World War II was over, Peace adopted a congregation in Oldenberg, Germany, through which names and addresses of those in need were received, and to whom packages were sent. Later, the congregation adopted nine Korean orphans and supported a church in Korea.

Peace was politically active as well. For example, in 1931 Peace sent a resolution to the Board of Regents of the University of California to support making military drill elective instead of compulsory. In 1937 Peace passed a resolution urging its congressman and senators to work for a neutrality law that would mandate an embargo on war materials. In September 1939 the church sent a telegram to President Franklin D. Roosevelt asking him "to give voice in your message tonight to a spirit of reconciliation in a world of gathering hate and destruction . . . help your fellow citizens to help the nations to find the way toward true unselfishness and good will, otherwise civilization will perish." In January 1940, the congregation officially became a peace church by amending its church constitution, article III, "Faith": "We are, as a Church, committed in every crisis to follow Jesus and under no circumstances to lend this church to war purposes."

The day after the December 7, 1941, attack on Pearl Harbor, Peace invited all the Japanese ministers of the area to meet with George Pacifist and Allan Everything to pray and prepare for the "dark days ahead." When the U.S. government forced Japanese Americans to leave their homes for relocation camps, Peace took legal ownership of a Japanese American Independent Church, maintained contact with the members while they were interned, and returned the church and their assets to them at the end of the war. The care of these members extended deeply. One member of Peace, for example, took care of a Japanese immigrant's family home during the war, rented it out for $35 per month and sent the proceeds to the family. No wonder the FBI shadowed Allan during the war!

The congregation included several conscientious objectors, in part a heritage of the pastoral leadership there since 1918. I had the privilege of interviewing one conscientious objector from World War II who was raised in the congregation and had spent the war fighting forest fires without pay. Peace not only supported all members who were conscientious objectors during the war; it also opened its church and parsonage for free housing and meals whenever a conscientious objector was in the area. Inevitably, some members supported the war efforts and others favored the pacifist position, but this division never split the church or caused people to leave Peace.

One of the former pastors of the Japanese American congregation whose assets Peace had cared for during World War II had returned to Japan and served a Methodist congregation in Hiroshima at the time of the atomic blast. He sent charred pieces of white camphor wood from Hiroshima to Peace as a symbol of peace and forgiveness from the Christians in Hiroshima. The wood was fashioned into a simple cross that Peace still uses.

Peace consistently served as a haven for all who sought to worship and become members, regardless of race, nationality, or creed. It prided itself on being the first congregation in the area to have African American members. In fact, I spoke to the first African American who came to Peace in the early 1930s as a nine-year-old boy and was a member by 1936. More than mere members, many African Americans, Asian Americans, and other people of color had a turn at every significant leadership position in the church, including an African American pastor. Peace was a fully integrated congregation by World War II.

A powerful preacher and writer, Allan Everything produced nine books, the most famous of which was also published in Spanish and Japanese. He also pioneered in marriage education, stressing counseling, and reading as a prerequisite to marriage. One of his books explored the possibilities of marriage. He was a popular speaker at college and young-adult conferences. He was known as a person of prayer and made prayer a part of almost every situation. From the start of the war and continuing many years after, George Pacifist and Allan Everything held a period of prayer and meditation at four P.M. every Saturday. By the 1930s (and during the Great Depression) Peace was large enough to have associate pastors. Until the early 1960s, people still filled the church at worship.

By the time Allan retired in 1963 at age 70, he and the congregation were well known in the area. After 45 years of powerful leadership under George Pacifist and Allan Everything, the congregation would have had difficulty finding any pastor to live up to its expectations. It is not surprising that problems arose after such long pastorates. What is surprising is the extent of the turmoil and disintegration.

The first sign of trouble came in the effort to call a new pastor. After 44 meetings in six months, the call committee recommended a candidate who was voted down by the congregation. Next, Peace considered the associate pastor, who had stayed on as acting pastor during the interim. Although he received a majority of the votes, he failed to receive the necessary two-thirds vote. A new pulpit (call) committee had to be formed; it eventually recommended Henry Cause, who was called.

Always controversial, Henry continued the activist traditions of his predecessors by going to Cuba in 1966 and to Vietnam in 1967. His sociopolitical stands brought much media attention to Peace, and Henry was invited to address major congregations throughout the nation and to talk with government officials in Washington. In that time, Peace tried innovations to church policies and practices, with the formation of an executive council and later a council of lay ministers. (Apparently the pastor and a few lay leaders ran the church.) The change, while satisfactory to many, caused others to feel too far removed from the church's decision-making base. Peace started many other endeavors, such as a Head Start program at the church, and a youth employment center. The pastor's vision of erecting a 100-to-300 apartment complex—senior citizen's housing in place of the present church property (placing the church on the top floor)—never came to pass, although Peace held several discussions about feasibility and cost. In the end, however, the pastor himself, his preaching, and his social activism proved too controversial, and finally the church split over his ministry. He was asked to leave in 1969, and many people followed.

As noted earlier, the church never really talked through the reasons for the termination and its subsequent impact on the church. Instead, Peace followed "the suggestion that as long a time as necessary be given to *finding just the right person*" (emphasis added). This person would be "someone with spiritual strength, a liking for people, with sensitivity and receptivity, with skills in relating to the community, a man with social vision." Because the church sought a clergy leader who possessed all these gifts, 21 months passed before Peace had a full-time pastor. By this point, Sunday attendance was down to about 100.

The next two pastors brought stability, strength, and good leadership. The first, the Rev. Dan Steadfast, from the Disciples of Christ, came in late 1970 and retired in 1984. He was still listed in the bulletin and on the Web page as pastor emeritus when I visited, although he and his wife held their membership elsewhere. By the 1970s, the urban area around the church was decaying, and no new growth occurred in the area.

During Steadfast's years, many urban churches near Peace closed their doors, but his ministry brought stability. Moreover, the congregation left behind a period of grief, discouragement, and defeatism, and became again a forward-looking, optimistic fellowship of Christians. During these years, Peace settled 22 refugees from Vietnam and cared for five members of a Cambodian refugee family. Volunteers from the church taught more than 100 people English as a second language. The music program, always well supported, remained strong with several concerts each year. Peace continued its activist nature by supporting farm workers in California and launching a nutritional senior lunch program for the community. Also during Dan's tenure, the cost of maintaining the building became too great a financial burden. As a result, Peace rented the building out to other congregations. In the 1970s, a Mandarin-speaking Chinese congregation that had rented worship and Christian education space at Peace grew strong enough to purchase its own building. By 1984, the tenant congregations were Korean, Thai, and Hungarian.

From 1985 until 1989, the first woman pastor, Penny Action, served this congregation. She was well liked, and more young adults joined the church. While the congregation voted against becoming a "sanctuary" church in 1985, later in her tenure it voted to become a "Just Peace" church. "Just Peace" denotes UCC congregations that have studied the issues and pledged themselves to be involved in the movement for peace and justice. Peace continued its activist tradition by participating in Central American issues, and by staging protest trips to Yucca Flats, a nuclear testing site where one congregational leader was arrested three times and Penny herself arrested once.

Then came the crisis years described earlier. While the congregation would eventually vote to end the tenure of John Independent (1991–1994), his tenure brought a positive outcome when Peace voted to become an "Open and Affirming" congregation—the UCC term for a church that welcomes people regardless of sexual orientation. However, in addition to the conflict with the pastor and the decline in worship attendance during these years, financial shortages became so great that the building and the organ began "to decline precipitously." The split between John and the congregation widened to the point that he was asked to resign in 1994. The next part-time interim ministry (1994–1996) ended in conflict and set the stage for calling Bee Love (1996–1998) as intentional interim minister. The UCC judicatory had recommended that Peace accept an intentional interim minister and gave the church two candidates from which to choose.

Intentional Interim Minister

One interviewee used sports terms to describe Bee's coming: She was a "relief pastor." He characterized her ministry as extremely significant because the church people were battered, bruised, and extremely discouraged. When the team was so beaten down, she was called in as a designated relief pitcher. "She rolled up her sleeves and told us we were important. She told us our church and its history have meaning and are worth fighting for," he said. "She committed a great deal of time to us, even though she was not staying for the long haul."

When Bee arrived, Peace was examining several options. The most drastic was to close the church, which members did not want but feared could happen. Another option considered seriously was to sell the building that had been such a financial drain, and to find a storefront or some similar location, or to merge with another congregation. In fact, leaders of Peace spoke with leaders of two other congregations. Peace rejected one as being more discouraged than Peace was, and the other church rejected the invitation because it was not ready to unite with an "Open and Affirming" congregation.

Adequate preventive maintenance had not been done on the church building for years. The sanctuary looked depressing, with paint peeling, carpet held together with duct tape, and a dark altar area. According to Bee, no healthy pastor would accept a call to a congregation whose building looked abandoned. Moreover, the clearest sign outside the church was for the Korean congregation that rented space in the church. The present pastor, Paul Proclaimer, and several recent members said they went by the church building many times and thought it was a Korean congregation. Bee arrived at a congregation in critical condition, doubtful whether it would survive. But she came well organized, with a plan of what to do and when to leave.

At the time of the interviews, Bee had been an intentional interim minister for almost 20 years and had completed 15 assignments. Of her 15 interim posts, she described 10 congregations as having a high level of conflict. Nine churches suffered from a pastor's sexual misconduct, and at eight a former minister was still hanging around and keeping the conflict going. Bee was a charter member of the Interim Ministry Network and a leader in that organization since 1985 as coordinator of training events. She herself had led some 35 different training events. It is no wonder that one of the interviewees said that Bee knew instinctively what was wrong and how to get the healing process started. Another said, "She was very clear about her role and understood the fact that she was interim and was going to leave, and the decisions were up to us."

Bee modestly said that the gift she brought was a fresh perspective. "The building looked abandoned and needed so much repair. I brought new eyes that held up a mirror and said, 'This is what you look like.'" A layperson said that Bee realized how very dismal the church building was and, once the members realized that they needed to fix it up, "She went through like a cyclone. She cleaned up the place."

In her initial interview, Bee told the leaders at Peace what she would do and how she could help them. And then she listened to them. Before Bee accepted the interim call, she worked with the congregation on her job description. According to Bee, the description covered the standard items, "but it also spelled out my working with the congregation on a developmental path. Part of the contract was their agreeing to work on the path, agreeing to be in worship and to be supportive of the policy." Bee was convinced that the congregation's desperation came in part because they were only "making do" (that is, trying to survive), and in the job description Bee made clear that she wasn't just going to "make do." Bee's efforts led to a theological theme for her interim ministry: "Choose life" ("I set before you life or death" [Deut. 30:15]). "They decided to seek life. I wanted to show them how to celebrate the life of God in the church."

Several interviewees called Bee an "amazing organizer." One of the things she did was restructure the congregation. "When I came, I counted 72 positions they had listed in the directory of leadership and by actual count there were approximately 46 members. They were exhausted. If you think you are to do all of this and can't, you don't want to come to church." Bee greatly simplified the church structure under a leadership council, and brought the bylaws up to date with this new structure.

Even more than admiring her technical expertise, the people valued her as a person, and her energy had opened, as one interviewee put it, a "deep energy" in the people. Bee was described as a lot of fun, a colorful person, a lovely woman of ingenuity, and a warm, uplifting spirit ready to support individual efforts. She was also said to be sensitive to the "big picture," great in one-on-one situations to find out what other people were thinking, and a consensus builder. She "was a presence at the church. You could drop in anytime and she was there. She gave hours to this church above what she was paid for." As a result, bright paraments decorated the altar, new paint gleamed in the sanctuary, new carpet freshened the décor, and many other projects "spruced up" the church building.

Bee was also "very frank and got to the root of the problems in Peace." Even though Peace had voted to be an "Open and Affirming" congregation under the last pastor, she sensed that the members might have trouble accepting a gay minister if one were called, and she devoted several sermons to the topic of what it meant to act as an "Open and Affirming" congregation. More than one interviewee thought she was very helpful in this regard. A gay member said, "Bee is the first person in my life who spoke from the pulpit and told me it was OK to be gay and that I was still loved by Christ and God." Though she couldn't know whom Peace would call at its next pastor, she realized that many of the potential candidates in this area were gay.

Bee sat with the search committee members until they completed the congregational profile, which included what Peace was looking for in its next minister. "It was clear that the last time they called someone, something went very wrong," Bee said. At first, they wanted to use a six-year-old profile, but Bee would not allow that. They worked hard on a new profile that became a step toward healing. Like other trained interim ministers, Bee thought that one sign of congregational health was the ability to select a minister who was appropriate the members. Evidence of their renewed health became apparent when they interviewed someone who was not a good match for Peace and had the strength to say no. According to Bee, "They had a sense of purpose; they understood that God was present and that God had a new vision for them."

Bee became, as one member put it, "the first glue to hold the church together." By the time she left, the congregation had a much more positive self-image. One interviewee said that it wasn't the self-image of the church that really had changed; it was the self-confidence. In her final newsletter in July 1998, Bee told the members, "We have done what we set out to do when I began as your interim minister . . . two and a half years ago." She called them gracious people and said that it would be hard to say good-bye. She told them that they had made a good start in reclaiming the church building by re-establishing the sacred space for worship, fixing up the church office, repairing stained-glass windows, and beautifying the grounds. When she came, about 20 members attended weekly—the secretary and her son, families with a total of 12 children, and some elderly members. By the time she left, weekly worship attendance had risen to 35 people a Sunday.

Vision

The interviewee who said that Peace's self-confidence had grown had a valid point. In its broadest expression, from the time of Dr. Pacifist, the overall mission of Peace was to follow the example of Jesus Christ. Pastor Allan Everything developed what he called "A Working Philosophy for Our Church." It read: "This church is a fellowship, a family, a team. What holds us together is our relationship with the Master and the task He gives us, both individual and social." Notice that Allan describes this as a philosophy, not a theology. More important, notice that this vision statement is not necessarily Christocentric. "The Master" can refer either to Jesus or to God the Creator. No reference is made to the saving death and resurrection of Jesus Christ. It points rather toward a relationship to God that resulted in following Jesus' example as lived during his earthly life.

Just before Bee arrived, the leadership developed a mission statement. Again, the statement was deliberately broad to encompass varying views of the mission. Notice, however, its great similarity to the Allan Everything philosophy:

> We love Jesus and seek to follow him. In this light, we strive to recognize and nurture the Christ in ourselves and in each stranger we meet along the Way. With this Love, we encourage all peoples of this church to pursue their individual passion: the struggle for peace with justice, the caretaking of our Mother Earth, the work with elders and youth, the vigil of prayer and meditation, the joy of song. In all these things and by the grace of God, we commit our life to the Sacred Spirit.

"This statement kind of reflects our theology," one member said. "We're not quite sure of the Jesus thing. We want to believe, but I wouldn't call us Christ- or Jesus-centered." Another interviewee, a member for only a few years, said that one of the attractions of this church was that one didn't get forced into narrow dogma. "I mean that I'm not ready to affirm the two natures of Jesus Christ, and that's OK here." Another said that while the mission statement reflects the members' views, it misses the central attractive force for the congregation: "The biggest thing is being open and accepting."

Finally, Peace Church also has a statement on the home page of its Web site—a statement that represents how the church wants to be seen by outsiders:

> Peace Congregational is an Open and Affirming, Just Peace Church of the United Church of Christ. We have been in our original church building since 1911. Our history has been devoted to peace and reconciliation for all persons. The cross that has

graced our altar for over fifty years is made from the charred embers of a tree from Hiroshima, and represents the church's long standing commitment to issues of justice, notably its fight against the internment of Japanese Americans during World War II.

We welcome all persons. We are the first integrated church in this city, and our membership represents a wide diversity of races, cultures, religious backgrounds, and sexual orientation.

Members of the congregation are the first to admit that they are not the church for everyone, but those seeking openness and acceptance, regardless of their circumstances, are welcome.

The Settled Pastorate

Following the interim, Peace called Paul Proclaimer. When Paul arrived in August 1998, he immediately settled on a theme to guide his ministry. Taken from the book by David Ray, *The Big Small Church Book* (Cleveland: Pilgrim, 1992), the theme is: "A church that knows who it is and why it exists will find the 'how' to fulfill its mission." In one of his first sermons that month, he elaborated on this theme.

There are two theological questions to be asked. What is our essential nature, and what is our essential purpose? A church that knows who it is and why it is, can then figure out how to be who and what it is. We know who we are. We know that in the face of religion for the status quo, we have always been an irritant. We know that in the chill of a high tech-world, we are low-tech with our warmth. We know that we look primarily at the gospel to the example of Jesus, and try to be every possibility we can be of that example's expression. We know who we are; we just need to be reminded.

Then, Paul turned to one of the members' greatest fears—that they would not have money to continue as a viable congregation—by quoting from Ray's book:

> Most churches think the biggest issue is fiscal—how to buy and
> pay for what they think they need. But the major issue is and
> always will be theological—how to be the kind of church God is
> calling us to be. The *sub-plot* is how to pay for it. But any church
> that knows who it is, and why it exists will figure out *how* to be
> what it wants to be.

This theme was mentioned not just in one sermon; Paul again and again
presented it for members of Peace to ponder.

Along with this theological theme, Paul advanced a subtheme about
how valuable a small church is. He repeatedly told the congregation that it
was exactly the size and the way it needed to be. In this powerful early
sermon he said that God has a bias for the small. Large congregations flex
their muscles and use their power to get what they want. But small churches
must rely on God's grace alone in the absence of clout.

> We are exactly the right church in exactly the right place at exactly
> the right time. We need to believe and know it. We are rooted
> deeply and have borne exactly the right fruit in every stand and
> every statement, and in our inward expression of community that
> keeps you the Spirit-filled people you are. Look at your church
> history in retrospect. If God is for us, then who can be against us?
> (Rom. 8:31).

These themes, frequently reiterated, burned themselves into the psyche of
the leadership of Peace. Paul also honored the people by celebrating their
history with a series of sermons emphasizing that this community of people
had, throughout their history, committed themselves to nonviolence and to
inclusiveness and respect for all human beings. According to one interviewee,
Paul said, "What you have always had in this church are people the world
had shut out or ignored, being brought into a community and told 'you really
are important.'"

When Paul arrived, he immediately went about working with
congregational members to establish their identity. Using the book by James
E. Birren and Donna Deutchman, *Guiding Spiritual Autobiography*
(Baltimore: Johns Hopkins University Press, 1991), he invited a sub-group
of 16 to develop a spiritual autobiography for Peace Church. He developed
a self-actualization chart by drawing a triangle on the board. The corners

were labeled "Our Real Self," "Our Ideal Self," and "How Others See Us." The congregants filled in each category ("Our Ideal Self" was divided into two areas: Building/Usage and Mission/Outreach). The result was an identity based on the three versions of the self. Even after the initial 16 made their report to the church, Paul invited others to work with him to further develop and refine the spiritual triangle. "As we discovered more about the 'autobiography' of the church, I invited members to comment on their own spiritual autobiographies, using the church's core values as a springboard," Paul said. "People work in groups of threes to talk about their own spiritual growth together, and help each other to develop a short 'talk' from this experience that they can stand in the pulpit and share with the congregation."

Paul next used the UCC Church Renewal Program to have members look for ways to integrate the ideas gathered from the spiritual autobiography to define the church's identity and reach out to the neighborhood around and beyond the church. At this point, Peace Church decided to move into long-range planning.

Who is Paul Proclaimer? Who is this person who came to Peace Church and developed themes and projects for renewal? Paul grew up on the East Coast wanting to be a minister from the time he was 11. He went off to college to become a minister, only to discover himself to be gay. He tried to deny his gayness but finally realized it was who he really was. For the next 12 years, he was an actor in New York, during which time he attended Riverside Church in Manhattan, where William Sloane Coffin was minister. In New York he met his life partner, Carl, another actor, with whom he has been together for 19 years.

In the mid-1980s, Paul and Carl decided to move to the West Coast, where Paul's next career was in interior design. In 1992, he and Carl formed a real estate agency. However, Paul's work did not satisfy or fulfill him, and in therapy he recovered his calling to be a pastor. With Carl's support, he entered a well-known West Coast United Methodist seminary. While in seminary, he reaffirmed the gifts he had for ordained ministry that he had kept submerged. He received his master of divinity degree with honors in 1997. He also received the Preaching Award, given to the student whose preaching is deemed most promising for pulpit ministry. On that occasion, the president of the seminary described him: "Paul is phenomenal and outstanding! He is articulate and organized. He gets things done. I would like to have him for my pastor."

During seminary he was licensed as a minister at First Congregational Church in the West Coast city where he lived. On June 1, 1997, he was formally ordained into the National Association of Congregational Christian Churches.

Paul had difficulty being placed because he was gay. When the time came for Paul to consider possible calls, a pastor saw fit to write area NACCC churches about Paul's sexuality and urge them not to call him. At one church, he became the nominee of the call committee, but failed to receive the necessary two-thirds affirmation.. The United Church of Christ was not initially eager to have Paul at Peace, since he was not a member of that denomination. He had, however, substituted once at Peace as Sunday morning worship leader and preacher for Bee during her interim ministry there. He made such an impression on the members that later, when the search committee was not satisfied with the candidates it had considered, it sought him out.

In Paul's response to the invitation from the search committee, he wrote in part: "Just so we don't waste each other's time needlessly, I would like to convey that I consider myself to be progressive and theologically liberal. I believe that God's greatest care and concern is for the poor and the marginalized, and I often preach a social gospel. I want to be in a diverse environment, and am looking for a pulpit from which to build a ministry." Paul also began fulfilling denominational requirements so that he could be accepted as a UCC minister.

During the week in which Paul was to be voted on by the entire membership, a brief anonymous letter was sent to all congregational members simply stating that Paul was gay. The writer expressed uncertainly as to whether this fact was known by all members. Perhaps because of this letter, before the congregational vote on Paul, the search committee asked him to introduce Carl to the congregation, and the members applauded his partner. The congregants then voted unanimously to make Paul their pastor.

The call was for three-quarters time, with the hope that Peace would be able to move to a full-time call within three years. Since full-time ministry was the goal of the congregation, Paul immediately told them that Peace would need at least 150 members, with 100 in weekly worship, to achieve this goal. Meanwhile, Carl's success as a real estate agent enabled them to live in this city where living costs are very high.

Paul also brought with him his deep engagement in two social-ministry arenas: he was on the board of directors of Hope-Net, a not-for-profit organization dedicated to eradicating hunger and homelessness. He asked the congregation to become involved with this organization, and, with other congregations in the area, to become a joint Foodlink Partner. Foodlink is the name given to a structure for gathering particular kinds of foods needed for food pantries. Paul also was on the institutional review board of AIDS Research Alliance, an organization working to test new drugs for those suffering with HIV/AIDS.

Paul ignored the often-quoted bromide to wait one year and get to know the congregation before making any changes. Bee had planted the hope that things could be done here, and Paul immediately sought to build on that foundation. Beyond the already described new endeavors he started in his first year, Paul continued cleaning, painting, and restoring the church building—an effort that Bee had begun. His previous work as an interior designer made it easy for him to lead in this area. And he always was willing to work alongside the members. If they were gathered to do some painting, Paul was painting with them. Giving an example, one member said, "He said when he came to help paint that he needed to leave by 1:00 P.M. to work on his sermon, but at two he would still be there. I can't say enough good things about Paul."

Among the interviewees, consensus emerged about the skills Paul brought. First, he was a strong leader, but also a good listener. Paul had a vision for Peace and, as one person said, "You don't have trouble seeing his vision." Paul remained candid with the congregation about what he wanted to see happen but did not force his point of view on the church. He was respected for this integrity, and most important, he became a consensus builder. As one person put it, "Paul brings people together toward a goal. He pushes us to do more than we usually do." He was able to set priorities and he "keeps things moving." Through it all, he maintained a sense of humor. Members agreed that he was a high-energy person, with a way of looking at the positive side of their situation. Underlying all these skills Paul loved and cared about people. He demonstrated his care and concern by getting to know personally every member of the congregation during his first year as pastor.

Paul also was able to reach all ages in the church, with particular skill in attracting new members in their 30s and 40s. When I visited, the church had more children than at any time in recent memory, and the members proudly pointed to the five babies in the church. At the same time, the old-timers were drawn to him as well. I was able to interview the "pillars" of the church, many of whom had been members for over 50 years, and universally, these members spoke appreciatively of Paul's ministry. For example, three members with a cumulative membership of over 220 years described Paul: "He has so much vitality and brings so much good out in everyone. We have a range of age groups, and he touches them all. Paul is very well organized. He is a wonderful preacher. We look forward to services."

Members saw worship leadership as another huge strength, as Paul put a lot of thought into every detail of each service. Further, members described his preaching as fantastic, extraordinary, and engaging. "He relates the stories and people in the Bible to real experiences today," said one interviewee. "He treats them in their historic context, and then he bridges that temporal gap and shows us how it makes our lives different today." Having had the opportunity to read several of his sermons and also to hear Paul preach, I can testify to Paul's powerful preaching both because of the content, his ability to craft a sermon and turn a phrase, and, as a former actor, his expressive delivery of the sermon.

Issues

The congregation struggled during the several years prior to my visit over what to do about the tenants who rented the church building. The congregation depended on the income to meet its budget. But renting had several consequences. First, Peace often could not use its own building because one of the tenants was using it. Second, signage made one think that it was exclusively a Korean church. (Paul later changed the signage so that Peace's sign was as large as that of the Koreans.) Third, one of the Latino congregations played such loud music late on Saturday nights that neighbors frequently complained, giving the church a negative image. Finally, some of the renting congregations did not take care of the property, and this fact greatly increased the upkeep costs.

Paul, using the building as a metaphor, told the congregation that members had not taken care of themselves, and the lack of self-care showed in the building. As the building was refurbished, Paul celebrated each accomplishment, making members see that they were beginning to take care of themselves again. Paul also believed that the lack of self-care allowed Peace to be "abused by the tenants." Since Paul's arrival, Peace had asked one tenant to leave because of destruction in the building. Another congregation left suddenly after objections over some restrictions in its use of the building. The loss of income meant that the congregation had to pick up the 20 percent of the budget that these rental agreements brought.

At the time of my visit, Paul indicated to the congregation that he was spending too much of his time acting as landlord. In this older church plant, something was always breaking. Negotiations for terms of rental or interviewing potential renters was left largely in his hands. The people worried about Paul's burning out as landlord. "We need to remove the responsibilities of running the building, so Paul can concentrate on the ministry," said one member. "We need to optimize his work." Another interviewee described the building as a drain. "It costs a lot of money to fix it up, and we don't have it. Paul spends 50 percent of the day managing the building, and he shouldn't have to do that."

Underlying the need for lay leaders to take responsibility for administering the building was the more general issue of developing lay leadership. Several members acknowledged that the church needed more lay leaders, especially among the new and younger members. Paul himself said that he often was put into the position of leading and doing, because no one else seemed to want to do it. He actively worked to develop lay leaders. As new members were received into the congregation, Paul recognized in some of them qualities that made them the perfect recruits for key leadership positions. However, he did not want to put brand-new congregants on the spot, realizing that they needed a year or so to acclimate to the church.

What was clearly not an issue was Paul's gayness. "We are a sign of the times with Paul being gay," said one member. "If you are not comfortable with a variety of lifestyles and multiethnicity, you can't live in this area," said another. Paul's partner, Carl, was active in the congregation and head of the committee on membership development. Carl and Paul lived like any other long-term married couple, and this congregation accepted them as they were. Nor had Paul's gayness been a disadvantage in bringing younger heterosexual couples and children into the congregation. People who might be turned off because the pastor was gay would also be turned off by the general liberalism of this congregation.

Future

In Paul's interview, he spoke about wholeness by reflecting on the biblical story of the man ill for 38 years who had never been healed because he hadn't gotten into the healing pool when it was stirred up (John 5:1-17). Reflecting on the character, Paul Proclaimer asked whether he really wanted to be healed. Then he made the bridge to Peace: "Do *we* really want to be healed? Do we want to be led from this barren place?" Clearly, Paul thought the people had shown since Bee's arrival that they did want to be led from the barrenness of their situation, characterized by the dilapidated church plant, but he knew it would continue to take a lot of prayer and work, and that the people could still become discouraged and give up.

When I visited, there was still fear that financial issues would overtake everything. Peace desperately needed a parking lot, since the only parking places were on the streets, and already occupied by cars belonging to residents. Members also wanted to escape from their financial dependence on groups renting their property; they set a goal to be independent by 2005. Weekly attendance was at 80 worshipers. Yet, the congregation needed to grow at least 25 percent in weekly attendance for the congregation to be able to pull this off. While several members expressed realistic optimism, another said, "I don't believe we've looked seriously enough at ourselves lately and what we have to do. We are still in the throes of euphoria of having Paul." Clearly, many hurdles remained.

On the other hand, Peace had a lot going for it. As the intern at the congregation put it:

> Peace is a community of people that has, both in its history and currently, committed itself to nonviolence and to inclusiveness and respect for all human beings. What you have here are histories of people, where the world would have shut them out or ignored them, being brought into this community and told, you really are important.

Asked to describe this congregation, one longtime member responded: "Deep love. Deep love for all people." Paul himself says that one of the reasons he thinks he meshes so well with this congregation is that "there is this outsider thing about the church and about me that fits well together."

Members were strongly committed to Peace. One member said, "Three things you can't talk about in this city: having a happy marriage, being proud to be a parent of your children, and where you go to church. I talk about Peace and am proud of it. . . . People are so passionate about this church and I don't see that changing." Other members pointed to the strong sense of family as evidenced in the fact that the coffee hour after worship lasted longer than the service itself. In fact, one member said that the next big hurdle for Paul and Peace would be maintaining a sense of smallness in a larger congregation.

As one interviewee looked to the future, she hoped they would again become "a beacon to the [metropolitan] community." In the meantime, Paul and the lay leaders faced the future confidently while remembering their past. In August 2001, Peace invited its sister Japanese American Church—the congregation Peace had helped during World War II—to a joint worship service on "Hiroshima Sunday." The church was specially decorated for the service, and a well-known Japanese American leader was the speaker. A front-page article in the major metropolitan newspaper where Peace is located commemorated the congregation, its inspiring history, and its present ministry. When this chapter was being written, the congregation was beginning to plan for the centennial of the church in 2005.

Conclusion

The Leadership Factor:
Key in Decline and Renewal

A ll the congregations described in this book were studied because they had experienced a major conflict that was addressed with the help of an intentional interim minister. Conflicts in churches are as diverse as the many congregations that worship and the leaders who shepherd them, so we should not expect a one-size-fits-all solution to the difficulties we encounter in our own settings. No *typical* congregation exists except in someone's mind, and no standard conflict can serve as the master model to which all conflicts can be compared. The message of the book is carried in the variety of stories told. That is, only by looking at specific examples of congregations in conflict can leaders be helped in anticipating and dealing with the crises in their own congregational settings. This observation leads to my first conclusion about the congregations I studied.

Models of Revitalization

1. The six congregational examples of revitalization are the basic point of this book. Humans learn best from examples. Reflecting on one way in which the Bible guides our spiritual lives, Martin Luther saw importance in the many stories of faithful men and women living before God. In his preface to the Psalter, for example, Luther pointed approvingly to the many legends of the saints, passionals, and books of examples in which the lives of the saints were set forth as lessons for devout Christians to follow. "We also find [in the Psalter] what all the saints still do, such as the attitude they take toward God, toward friends and enemies, and the way they conduct themselves amid all dangers and sufferings" (*Luther's Works*, American edition, E. Theodore Bachman, ed., 35:254, 1960). He preferred the Psalter above any other compilation of examples because of the depth of insight into lives of the saints. The Psalter "lays before us not only their words instead of their deeds, but their very hearts and the inmost treasure of their souls, so we can look down to the foundation and source of their words and deeds" (*Luther's Works*, 35:255).

The stories of faithful people living before God inform our faith journey, but equally helpful are the Bible's accounts of people acting in unsaintly ways. The Bible records God's people fleeing from God, arguing with God, forgetting God, raging against God. and rebelling against God—precisely the things we do! Because we learn so much from examples, much preaching today is not didactic but narrative, telling the stories of contemporary saints and sinners as good or bad examples for us. Just so, this book has presented six living examples of congregations being revitalized by turning away from decline and death to health and mission.

Growth amid Decline

2. Faithful and skilled intentional interim ministers and subsequent faithful and skilled settled pastors demonstrate that robust, trustworthy, growing ministry can occur even when the area around the church is in a stable or declining phase of its life cycle. None of the six churches studied is located in a growing neighborhood. Just as congregations are living organisms subject to a life cycle, so also are neighborhoods and entire communities. Neighborhoods emerge, develop, and become stable, and congregations tend to follow their neighborhood's cycle. All six congregations grew rapidly when their section of the community boomed. Thus, Peace Congregational grew between the 1920s and the 1950s; Household Presbyterian grew in the 1950s and 1960s; Reasonable Baptist grew through the 1970s when new housing in the area of the church was largely saturated.

Without renewal, eventually neighborhoods or communities decline. This decline can take many forms, from the whole community losing population (for example, the area where Established United Methodist is located) to a shift in neighborhood demographics toward more ethnically diverse, poorer, and more transient residents—not typical members of mainline denominations. Older, declining urban neighborhoods sometimes renew themselves through gentrification. The area around Peace

Congregational had been undergoing a modest regentrification in the past decade, and the neighborhood around Household Presbyterian was just beginning to regentrify itself. These changes don't bring about an increase in population but often result in new neighbors who might be more inclined to attend mainline Protestant churches.

Just as congregations tend to follow their neighborhood as it moves through the growth and stabilization phase of its life cycle, they also tend to follow the downswing. Established United Methodist declined as the whole town declined, for example. Reasonable Baptist is in a somewhat different situation. Though Reasonable's immediate neighborhood is becoming more commercialized rather than growing, the wider surrounding area is expanding rapidly in population. To tap this growth in the wider area, Reasonable has had to redefine itself from a city-neighborhood congregation to a regional church reaching a tri-county area. Though Reasonable had not been a strictly neighborhood church for many years, until the current pastor arrived it still served largely the area near the church. Only in its rebirth under the present pastor was it able to reach out to the population in the three-county area.

Because of the life-cycle changes in the communities around them, four congregations in particular—Household Presbyterian, Established United Methodist, Peace Congregational, and Majestic Episcopal—became made up largely of elderly people, leading the members to fear that their churches might die soon without younger members to take over. This anxiety put pressure on every pastor to reverse the trend of decline in the community and church. Moreover, as we saw in these congregations, churches concerned about their own survival tend to focus upon themselves and demand that pastors meet their internal needs first, rather than keeping the focus on the mission outside the church. In other words, although the crises in each of the churches derived from specific causes, the pressure of the life cycle of the community and the resulting graying of the church provided an underlying environment in which a crisis could occur. The six congregations studied overcame not only negative neighborhood changes but also internal church crises.

Sometimes a congregation's focus on its "glory days" can keep it in the valley of despair and in desperate need of revitalization. At Peace, Majestic, and Adrift, the life cycle of their neighborhoods peaked at the same time that a nationally known pastor or internationally known church leader provided leadership for the congregations. Today all that has changed, and their glorious histories threatened to be a millstone dragging the congregations down rather than a balloon lifting them into the future. That these congregations did not remain museums to the past is a mark of the faithful vision for the future carved out by the interim ministers, the settled pastors, and the laity themselves.

The Effect of Leadership Choices

3. *Certain pastoral leadership choices, styles, and behaviors lead a congregation to a decline in mission and participation by members.* The insight that pastors play a pivotal role in the health of a congregation is not new. The research for this book confirms that insight and suggests some reasons why it is true. When we look at the study congregations, we might well wonder whether the fact that a church is in decline leads both the pastor and congregation to make poor decisions about their ability to work together. Perhaps the pastors think they can "save" the church. Perhaps the congregations are desperate to be "saved." Neither is thinking clearly about the realities of the situation at hand. Mismatches also sometimes occur because of a congregation's poor self-image: "We don't deserve anyone better matched to us than this pastor." Or, the church does not learn enough about the pastor's leadership style before issuing the call.

In four of the six congregations, a mismatch between pastor and parish sparked a crisis severe enough to threaten the stability of the congregation. Majestic, Peace, Household, and Established all reported that their crises erupted when the expectations of pastor and parish failed to synchronize. The congregations probably should not have issued a call to those pastors.

The pastors themselves must also shoulder some of the blame for the mismatch, because they were not adaptable to the specific needs of the congregations. Some behaviors would land a pastor in trouble in almost any call. If a mark of creative leadership is the ability to adapt to each unique congregational setting, so rigidity in the pastoral office severely cripples such leadership. Other common complaints about pastors who lead parishes into crisis revolve around an overlapping set of behaviors such as lack of visibility at the church, absence of office hours, inability of congregants to get in touch with the pastor, and insufficient visitation with the hospitalized, sick, and shut-ins. Clearly, difficulties in forming meaningful relationships caused the greatest dissatisfaction with the pastors.

The stories of these six congregations show that it is not enough for a pastor simply to have a pleasing personality; he or she also needs definite skills for leading a church in troubled times. At Established, for example, Sandra Dodge was well liked, but interviewees said she lacked the leadership skills needed for her expanded position. About another pastor, one interviewee simply said that the "Peter Principle" was evidenced in his ministry—the concept that a person is promoted one level above her or his competence (Laurence J. Peter and Raymond Hall, *The Peter Principle* [New York: William Morrow, 1969]).

Another issue that leads congregations into crisis is open conflict between the senior pastor and a key individual or group in the congregation. We see such conflict between the senior pastor and associate pastor at Moderate, between the pastor and retired pastor at Adrift, and between the minister and powerful groups in Established, Majestic, and Peace. Conflict among staff or within a congregation shows a lack of adaptability on the part of all participants, especially the pastors. When conflict spills into the open, especially when it is so severe that nonmembers in the community learn of the problems and pray for a reconciliation, the crisis requires an extended period for healing and turning toward the future. Because of the open conflict at Established and Reasonable, the turnaround took longer, and at Adrift the revitalization may take even longer—if it ever arrives.

"If everyone would just learn to adapt and get along, everything would be fine" is a simplistic statement, to be sure. But I'm speaking about conflict based on a lack of respect for the other and a manner of conversing that polarizes people instead of drawing them closer. When one party does not respect another party as beloved brothers and sisters in Christ—when open communication is deliberately thwarted by lies and half-truths, when opponents are labeled rather than seen as complex individuals, when attempts are made to gather people to one side and against another—then a crisis of colossal proportions will inevitably occur.

The Perils of a Long Pastorate

4. *Some issues requiring the guidance of an interim pastor inevitably follow a long pastorate.* Many church leaders now define "long" pastorates as those that extend for 15 years or more. In our research, we examined two congregations where a pastor had served for more than 35 years. I

think the following principle is usually true: The longer a pastor serves a parish (especially longer than a generation), the more a congregation tends to find its identity in the pastor and his or her vision of ministry. After more than 25 years with one leader, most parishioners don't remember when the current pastor *wasn't* their leader. In some cases, the congregation tends to become known less for being Christ's church and more for being the long-term pastor's church. When the long-term minister establishes the identity of the congregation largely around himself or herself, as happened at Adrift, the crisis when that pastor leaves, retires, or dies is the most severe.

Two of the congregations illustrate the crisis that can occur after a long, productive pastorate. Peace Congregational's crisis came after Allan Everything retired in 1963, and Adrift Lutheran's crisis followed the retirement of Karl Opportune after 42 years. Even if the long-term pastor moves away, as Pastor Everything did, his or her longtime status as *the* pastor makes it almost impossible for anyone else to minister with success. Yes, there were specific, serious problems in the ministry of the pastor who followed Pastor Everything, but in the eyes of parishioners few, if any, pastors would measure up to Pastor Everything. Furthermore, as we saw at Adrift, when the retired pastor has wrapped the identity of the church around himself, and then stays in the congregation and wants to continue in a leadership capacity, the ingredients for an explosive crisis are present.

This study points up two other problem factors that sometimes follow the retirement of a longtime senior pastor. One is the presence of long-term professional staff who remain when the senior pastor retires. In two churches this became a potential issue. Bob Friend of Adrift stated it well himself: "I have been here a long time; I am a new pastor's worse nightmare." Bob understood that he might represent to the new senior pastor the old way of ministry, not the new leadership style of the new pastor. Yet the longtime associate often has the allegiance of the members of the congregation, and so can potentially undermine the ministry of the new senior pastor if disagreements arise. To Bob's credit, he recognized this potential problem: "I don't want to be a nightmare for the pastor, and I struggle with that."

Second, problems can arise not only from associate clergy, but also from longtime professional and support staff. This study uncovered secretaries so loyal to the former pastor that they had difficulty working with the new minister. Moreover, a large professional staff may have a vested interest in keeping the ministry going the way it has in the past, which the new pastor may understand not to be best for the present and future. Often when I work in the church, I think of these lines from James Russell Lowell's hymn text "Once to Every Man and Nation":

> New occasions teach new duties,
> Time makes ancient good uncouth . . .

How often in the church we forget that what might seem appropriate to one leader for yesterday and today seems "uncouth" to a new leader for today and tomorrow.

Interim Duties

5. *The three essential tasks of the intentional interim minister are (1) to reduce the level of conflict; (2) to assist the congregation with its self-identity; and (3) to help the church set goals for the future.* Charles Goodhart, intentional interim at Moderate, expressed these three aims, and I think they are the essential tasks of any intentional interim. I am aware that the Interim Ministry Network has traditionally described five developmental tasks, not three:

1. coming to terms with history;
2. discovering a new identity;
3. fostering leadership changes during an interim;
4. renewing denominational linkages; and
5. committing to new directions in ministry.

While the intentional interims I interviewed incorporated aspects of all five developmental tasks, they tended to break them down into three segments as Goodhart has listed them.

The first task is to reduce the conflict. This step requires the willingness of the parishioners to work hard at reconciliation. We saw this necessity demonstrated at every site, through many extra small-group meetings with emotionally draining conversations, surveys and other written instruments to complete, and additional congregational meetings. The leadership of each congregation took on enormous extra duties during the transition. Bee Love, intentional interim at Peace, asked the congregation to commit to the requisite hard work and to support the process before she would even sign her job description. That is to say, Bee made her job description into a kind of covenant between herself and the congregation, with responsibilities on each side. Bee asked the members to commit to and support the developmental path, and to attend worship.

Each intentional interim recognized the critical point made by Charles Goodhart, that the interim period is a process, not a program. Rather than be enslaved to doing the same thing in every congregation, the seven intentional interims customized their plan to the particular conflict and needs of the church to which they were called. Thus, people remarked on the interims' general level of expertise as much as on the specific steps through which the interims led them to reduce the conflict level. However, parishioners usually meant by expertise the interims' ability to adapt themselves and their ministry to the particular needs of each congregation. In church after church members remarked that the interims were "very clear in their role and know how to get healing started," or that "the interims knew their role and its boundaries." In other words, their presence was reassuring to the congregation because the congregants could put their trust in the process. Moreover, almost every interim was described as a leader who listened and communicated well—two essential components for any leader, especially in a crisis. It helped greatly that most of the intentional interims had a wonderful sense of humor and did not take themselves too seriously, or let the congregation meet without seeing the humor in certain situations.

As the intentional interims gathered the congregants into small groups to give them the opportunity to talk about grief and anger, a few things stood out. One, the interims insisted that all issues be talked about freely and that nothing be swept under the rug. Second, besides asking people to listen to others without interrupting and always being civil in all comments, interims insisted on confidentiality of all that occurred in the small groups. The issues would be made public to the whole congregation, but who made specific comments would not be disclosed. In some congregations this small-group work was very structured (for example, the listening mission study at Household), whereas it was much more informal in others (such as at Peace). Finally, a time line (such as that used at Reasonable Baptist) on which the parishioners were invited to write positive notes about the history of the church and important components in their own lives provided an excellent avenue to help members realize why the church was important to them.

Because of the severe crisis in each congregation, almost every interim recognized the need to affirm the discouraged people. At Household, Pam Strong told them, "You are the best-kept secret in town." At Majestic, Norman Competent wrote, "I have been amazed at all the strengths that I am observing among you." At Peace, Bee Love saw herself as the designated relief pitcher sent to people who were battered, bruised, and extremely discouraged. First, she told the congregants that they were unique, with a unique ministry worth fighting for. Next, she invited them to "choose life." The members of all these congregations responded positively to the affirmation of the gifts they possessed and the promise of what could be tomorrow.

The intentional interims also brought a gift of administration to their calls. In site after site, interviewees described how the interim organized the membership rolls (some called it cleaning up the parochial records), and developed job descriptions for the staff or for standing committees. At Peace, Bee Love restructured the church leadership plan. All the interims were described as well organized, and sometimes even extremely organized. Our group of interims also possessed good computer skills, and a few of them revamped the office work and brought the congregations into the computer age. A congregation well managed is less likely to be in conflict.

As part of their ministry of administration, the interims brought fresh eyes to help the congregation look at the physical appearance of the church and grounds and to help them in sprucing up the church property, both inside and outside. The interims held up a mirror for the congregants to see themselves as outside visitors might and brought that awareness to help them examine every area of church life—from worship and fellowship to the signs outside. Again, when congregants take pride in the property, it shows that they value the congregation, its members, its mission, and its pastors in ways that will help them move past the present plight.

The first step of the intentional interim is very different when a beloved pastor of more than a generation retires, dies, or leaves. Here the first task, instead of reducing the level of conflict in the congregation, is to give the members time to grieve the loss of their minister. Congregations usually seriously underestimate the length of time it takes for the grieving to run its course so that the members can begin to turn their attention from their much-loved previous pastor to a new day under new leadership.

The second task of the interim is to clarify the identity of the congregation in crisis. In the process of reducing the conflict, interims helped members see how the church might be clinging to an identity appropriate for the past but not realistic for today. And so the intentional interims sought to help parishioners clarify who they were as a group and where they wanted to be. Paul Proclaimer, at Peace Congregational, quoted David Ray: "A church that knows who it is and why it exists will find the 'how' to fulfill its mission." At Reasonable Baptist, Charles Goodhart had the members trace the history of the congregation on a time line. Then he formed a denominational relationship subcommittee whose members heard presentations on "How Baptists Came to Be" and "How Baptists Are Today." This committee had as its goal "to determine the denominational identity of our church." At Established United Methodist, the intentional interims encountered a congregation that was rooted in United Methodist tradition, so they could focus on the denomination's *Book of Discipline* to help with identity and mission.

At Adrift the situation was more complicated. A threefold task needed to be undertaken: (1) to teach the leaders how to be leaders; (2) to help the congregation learn its identity; and (3) to teach the congregants what it means to be a Lutheran church. Also, Adrift was so large and the divisions so great that Mark Empower, the intentional interim, needed to work first with the leaders to help them form an identity as leaders (remember, he scheduled a retreat for the church council with an outside facilitator) before he could address the identity issues of the entire congregation. Helping the congregation understand its identity—and putting that in a biblical, theological, historical, and denominational framework—was important for both the intentional interims and the pastors who followed.

Clarifying and establishing an identity requires a laborious, demanding process. It was not surprising that in the middle of the task, some members, especially at Adrift, grew weary and wanted to be told the answers. The analogy to the Israelites wandering in the wilderness is apt here. "Either let us go back to Egypt where we can at least eat meat [that is, let us return to the way we used to do things], or take us to the Promised Land quickly where we can find a real leader to make us flourish again" (see Exodus 16). This sentiment points out a critical function of intentional interims. They help ease the panic of transition and the accompanying frenzy to find the perfect next pastor as soon as possible. Without interims, most parishes faced with a pastoral vacancy want to rush the process of calling a new settled pastor. Intentional interims help stop this panic, allowing the congregations time to bring out and heal the pain, establish an identity appropriate for a new pastor, and decide what gifts they want in a new pastor. All six of our churches learned this lesson.

The third task is to help the members set congregational goals for the future, which includes helping them learn what gifts they want in their next pastor. This task grows immediately from not rushing the transition. Even at Adrift, where many people were impatient with the length of the interim period, one member said, "Mark has helped us slow down and helps us do tasks by educating us with the way it should be done. His basics are to slow down, redefine our mission, and develop a clearer idea of what the church is looking for." There is a lot of truth in saying that one mark of a good intentional interim process is the subsequent ability of the congregation to choose an appropriate settled pastor. This book provides four examples in which congregations that had been in crisis did exactly that.

In these six parishes I also learned that developing lay leadership is a key step along the way to prepare a congregation to call the next settled pastor. At Adrift, Mark said his initial question to the leaders was "How can we come together and model the body of Christ?" That is, how can we be effective leaders so that this church can live faithfully as the body of Christ? At Established, Judy Moderator and Marge Verve insisted on involving members in decisions and delegating much of the ministry, even though the congregants sometimes complained about having to do too much work. Developing lay leadership helped prepare for the new minister to come.

Interims would ruin the healing they had accomplished had they then opened themselves to be permanently called to the congregation. It takes fresh leadership that has not been through all the transition battles to complete the revitalization of the congregations. As the final mark of excellent leadership, intentional interims know when to say good-bye and never succumb to invitations to become candidates for the settled pastorate. In some of the six congregations studied, an interim (but not intentional) ministry had begun well but ended in disaster by splitting the parish over whether the interim could be a candidate for the settled pastorate. Because intentional interims are clear that under no circumstances will they become permanent pastors, they can undertake the three essential tasks with no strings attached. Paraphrasing a biblical account (Matt. 12:43-45), we may say that such a betrayal would leave the congregation seven times worse than when the interim arrived. Like Moses, interims lead the people to the promised land and then step aside.

Building on the Interim Pastor's Work

6. Settled pastors can build on the foundation laid by the intentional interim ministers when they exhibit transparent faith, good communication skills, the ability to develop a vision with specific steps to carry it out, the adaptability to fit with the congregation, and high energy. Interviewees at the four congregations where a settled pastor had been called to follow the intentional interims said that these pastors exhibited readily apparent faith.

At Household, members said that Fiona Faith was "at peace with God and with herself," and that "she does what she does through the grace of God, who lives in her." At Majestic, the people said the pastor "does well in his own skin." In all four cases, the people said these pastors were open to God and open to people. The very foundation of their ministry lay in their transparent faith.

All these pastors were good communicators. At Peace, I gave the pastor the pseudonym "Paul Proclaimer" because of his ability to craft a sermon and his superb skill at delivery. In fact, I could have named all four ministers "Pastor Proclaimer," because all took preaching seriously and were excellent at it. Just as important, they wrote well. We saw that two of the four, Chuck Gregarious and Michael Excel, had previously been reporters or had majored in journalism at college. All four understood the paramount importance of proclamation and communication and took the time and made the extra effort to make sure that these things were done well.

All four pastors possessed a vision for the congregation. This does not mean that they imposed a vision upon the parishioners, but that pastor and lay leaders could combine their insights toward a mutual vision for the church. Remember, for example, that when Paul Proclaimer was first approached by Peace, he wrote the congregation a letter that said in effect, "Here is who I am, and here is the direction of my ministry. I don't want to waste my time or yours if you are going in a different direction." Peace saw that his direction was in all essentials the direction in which they wanted to go. Because of their communication skills, pastors helped congregants capture the vision and devise practical steps to reach it.

In all four churches, part of the vision involved building up the church through small groups, and this was true in the small churches as well as the large. For example, at Household, Fiona Faith used the choirs as small groups (especially the developing children's choir) and she started the young-adult group, the Seekers, as a cornerstone small group in the church. Because these pastors are leaders with vision, not all of these attempts succeed. As we saw, sometimes the vision had to be modified, or parts of it even given up, at least for the present. But the very willingness of these pastors to keep trying new things helps make them effective leaders.

Every pastor established a priority of developing younger lay leaders while simultaneously keeping engaged the older, longtime members (who also were the most generous givers). Yes, at each church there were a few people who sat back and waited to see what would happen with the new minister. But one key to the flourishing ministry at these four churches was the ability of these pastors to inspire younger lay leaders and keep the longtimers engaged.

In mission, outlook, and abilities, all four pastors adapted themselves well to their congregations. The good arose not by accident, but because the pastors and congregations were envisioning ministry in similar directions—all adapted themselves to the other. Two of these congregations had, before the present pastors were called, turned down a candidate who would not adapt as well to the congregation. Think how Michael fit at Reasonable Baptist because he was a moderate himself. Also, note that at the time Michael was called, the leaders at Reasonable were looking for "a young person with a passion for mission." Michael adapted to the changed needs of this congregation from his first call by developing with congregational leaders the contemporary worship service, The Open Door. Michael adapted in this way because the primary stated mission of this congregation was "to bring non-Christians to a saving relationship with Jesus Christ through participation in the community of the faithful (Reasonable Baptist Church)." His leadership took a different form in this call than in his first because of different circumstances.

Adaptability is not a sufficient leadership quality. It must be coupled with the ability to develop a vision and map out the specific steps to reach toward that vision. Adaptability by itself can be a dangerous response on the part of either the minister or the congregation. A pastor who wants simply to adapt may try to meet all the needs of the parishioners. Since people's felt needs are infinite, the pastor may end up exhausted, frustrated, angry, and approaching burnout, while the congregation, becoming increasingly more demanding, wonders why the church is stagnating or dying.

Notice that in all six congregations the leaders did much more than simply adapt. Early on, each intentional interim laid concrete plans to confront the crises, the divisions, and the pain they saw. In essence, the interims insisted that a "lancing of the boil" take place. They would not allow the hurt and pain to continue festering. They insisted that parishioners give quality time and great spiritual and emotional effort to confront the divisions among them. Most of all, the intentional interims were acute listeners, able to identify with the congregants in their pain and yet remain objective enough to bring a fresh outside perspective.

Likewise, the settled pastors who followed the interims needed to mold a vision congruent with the identity of the congregation but also to develop the vision further than could been done under the interims. One interviewee described this leadership style as the ability of the pastor to color outside the box, while keeping one hand on the box. Our four leaders showed not only how to expand the vision of the congregations but also how to develop strategies so that the vision could begin to be lived out.

All four of these settled pastors happened to be lively people. At Household, the interviewees said Fiona was a "high-energy and most enthusiastic Christian." The people of Majestic suggested that Chuck was like an Alka-Seltzer whose great imagination kept bubbling out. At Reasonable, Michael was compared to a talented juggler who could keep an incredible number of plates (ministries) in the air. Finally, Paul at Peace was paid for a three-quarter position. *No one* I talked to suggested that he *worked* only three-quarter time. In fact, all four worked hard, kept posted hours, and were available to their congregations.

I'm certainly not suggesting that pastors who want to revitalize congregations have to be workaholics. In fact, all four of the pastors established good boundaries for the sake of their own spiritual, mental, emotional, and physical well-being. Each took time for their families, time for retreat, reflection, and prayer, and each took his or her day off. But in the hours they worked as pastors, they worked with great energy and effectiveness. The high energy and the way it helped congregants to be enthusiastic led to an observation uttered at Household but applicable to all four sites: "Our glass could be seen as half-empty or half-full. We see it as half-full and filling."

The Importance of Intentional Interims

7. *Intentional interim ministers are critical components of church revitalization.*

A fair question to ask about the congregational accounts in this book is this: "Is it necessary to have *intentional* interim ministers in these congregations? Can't others (retired pastors, those without special training) accomplish the same ends? In answer I point to the specific skills the intentional interims have developed to release the congregations from their focus on the past— the divisions, the hurts, the frustrations—and turn the churches to the future. Not many ministers without special training are able to do this. Moreover, in some of the six sites an untrained interim minister had earlier been placed in these congregations in crisis, and healing did not occur.

However, this book presents no statistical data to argue for the superiority of intentional interims. In fact, training to be an intentional interim minister is no guarantee of effectiveness. A few pastors so trained may be looking for a way to stay in ordained ministry when they realize they don't have the gifts needed for settled pastorates (of course, they don't have the gifts to be intentional interims either). Also, a few very wise, capable pastors can become effective interim ministers by the trial-and-error method of learning on the job. For example, in the late 1960s, a retired pastor had served as an effective interim in the parish that became my first call. But for the most part, the competence of the intentional interims I encountered and the fruit of their special training led to a quality of leadership in the aftermath of a crisis and the resignation or retirement of the pastor that could not be accomplished by someone untrained.

The evidence presented by the examples of intentional interim ministers chronicled in this book leads me to state the following principle that I think, on the basis of my research and experience, to be true: *The more severe the crisis, the greater the need for an intentional interim minister.* One reason lies in the opportunities and challenges arising in a time of pastoral vacancy, different from any other point in the life cycle of a congregation. As Yon, Mead, and others have been pointing out for more than a generation, the parish between pastors inevitably faces changes and is at a "teachable moment" when the church is more open to innovation than otherwise. Churches must be at the point that they are willing to change, if intervention is to have much impact.

Intentional interims tailor their training and their ministry to pastoral vacancies, and they understand this juncture in a congregation's life as few others do. Moreover, most intentional interims have served at this crossroad in place after place. From experience as well as training, they anticipate what happens in transitions, especially if there was a crisis before the pastoral vacancy, or a vacuum because a pastor who had served a church for many years had left or retired. Intentional interim ministers know what to do in this situation. Most of us don't.

In sum, this book has at least provided examples of seven intentional interim leaders and four settled pastors who undertook a daunting challenge in ministry—revitalizing a parish—and flourished. Revitalizing a congregation is never easy. In the life cycle of a parish, when a church stops forming new groups, and other evidences of excitement and growth fail to appear, and when fatigue among the lay leaders and pastor follows, then the congregation is in need of renewal. The data mentioned in the introduction suggest that less than half the congregations undertake this renewal. Churches can remain in this stage of lethargy for many years with the possibilities of renewal becoming less likely each year until a crisis occurs.

The crisis often indicates just how far the congregation has declined, and the situation calls for a much more radical response than renewal. It calls for the revitalization of the congregation. Even a smaller percentage of congregations are willing to undertake the difficult work of revitalization than are willing to engage in renewal. Many a congregation in crisis find ways to apply adhesive bandages and continue to limp along as a lukewarm Christian church until a crisis erupts again. A few churches have the courage to allow themselves, with God's help, to be revitalized.

I have had the pleasure to present four parishes that have done well at the task of revitalization. We can learn from each one. Moreover, much can be learned from Established, where the signs of revitalization are all present but where the future depends on how the gifts of the next pastor match the needs of the congregation. We also learn from Adrift: we simply don't know where the church will go in the future, although beginning signs suggest that it also may be revitalized. These six congregations present wonderful examples and lessons about the ministry of revitalization. Countless stories of revitalization of churches like the ones in this book could be told, and many bear witness to the theme of death and resurrection that God has implanted in all living organisms.

Welcome to the work of Alban Institute...
the leading publisher and congregational
resource organization for clergy and laity today.

Your purchase of this book means you have an interest in the kinds of information, research, consulting, networking opportunities and educational seminars that Alban Institute produces and provides. We are a non-denominational, non-profit 25-year-old membership organization dedicated to providing practical and useful support to religious congregations and those who participate in and lead them.

Alban is acknowledged as a pioneer in learning and teaching on *Conflict Management *Faith and Money *Congregational Growth and Change *Leadership Development *Mission and Planning *Clergy Recruitment and Training *Clergy Support, Self-Care and Transition *Spirituality and Faith Development *Congregational Security.

Our membership is comprised of over 8,000 clergy, lay leaders, congregations and institutions who benefit from:
- ❖ 15% discount on hundreds of Alban books
- ❖ $50 per-course tuition discount on education seminars
- ❖ Subscription to *Congregations*, the Alban journal (a $30 value)
- ❖ Access to Alban research and (soon) the "Members-Only" archival section of our web site www.alban.org

For more information on Alban membership or to be added to our catalog mailing list, call 1-800-486-1318, ext.243 or return this form.

Name and Title: _____

Congregation/Organization: _____

Address: _____

City: _____ Tel.: _____

State: _____ Zip: _____ Email: _____

BKIN

The Alban Institute
Attn: Membership Dept.
7315 Wisconsin Avenue
Suite 1250 West
Bethesda, MD 20814-3211